D1447854

**A Method for Measuring
Decision Assumptions**

172

The MIT Press
Cambridge, Massachusetts,
and London, England

**A Method for Measuring Decision Assumptions**     Jarrod W. Wilcox

Copyright © 1972 by
The Massachusetts Institute of Technology

This book was designed by The MIT Press Design Department.
It was set in IBM Century
printed on Decision offset
by The Maple Press Company
and bound in Interlaken AV 1-892 Matte
by The Maple Press Company
in the United States of America.

Library of Congress Cataloging in Publication Data

Wilcox, Jarrod W. 1943–
    A method for measuring decision assumptions.

    Bibliography: p.
    1. Decision-making — Mathematical models.    I. Title.
HD69.D4W46                          658.4'033                          72-2890
ISBN 0-262-23055-0

To Linda

# Contents

Contents

## Preface and Acknowledgments

This book is meant to help find out why people make some choices rather than others. It asks of its reader some basic knowledge of statistical methods. Since it cuts across normally separate fields, it requires an adventuresome spirit. In return, one may expect to gain a tool of broad and varied uses in his own social science research and practical projects.

The message is on two levels. On one, the book is a practical handbook for application. On the other, it discusses fundamental issues in the theory of decision-making and the social sciences.

The work reported in this book was begun with the encouragement of Professors Zenon S. Zannetos and Mason Haire of the Alfred P. Sloan School of Management, M.I.T. Not only during the course of the research proper but over the past several years, Professor Zannetos has contributed greatly to my thinking regarding the analysis of planning and control processes. Professor Haire also strongly influenced the direction of this work through his contagious fascination with the differences among people in their perceptions of social situations. To Professor Hayward Alker of M.I.T.'s Political Science Department, special thanks are due for his wholehearted intellectual support in attacking the problem of statistical modeling of decision assumptions and the associated research design to test the method chosen.

The skills of Mrs. Eva Norman and Miss Janet Allen were indispensable in preparing the typed manuscript.

Once again, Professor Zannetos proved especially helpful to the work by providing editorial comments.

Finally, I wish to thank forty anonymous stock market participants for their very fine cooperation as experimental subjects.

# I

# Measuring Decision Assumptions

# 1        The Problem

Discovering reasons behind choices is a problem that is always with us. Yet, we rarely notice it clearly. Do the following plights have any features in common?

A young man seeking social relationships is distressed because young women of the type he finds most attractive lose interest in him quickly. He has only vague notions as to the reason for their rejections.

During a recession, a Detroit auto designer needs to know whether the public really prefers small cars or is just buying smaller cars because of falling disposable income.

A major political party wishes to construct a party platform likely to unseat the opposition in next year's vote.

An intelligence expert finds that the new policy-makers pay little heed to his reports. Despite this, they blame him for not having warned them when crises occur.

A large government program to aid the economic progress of minority groups by funding new business ventures is wasting money. The head of the program wants to know if successful and unsuccessful entrepreneurs differ in the ways they think about the problems of running their firms.

A manager asks himself how much responsibility it is wise to delegate to his new assistant.

A psychiatrist wants to identify more definitely patients likely to attempt suicide. Over the years he has gained an instinctive skill in this. Instinct, however, is hard to analyze and improve upon.

A modestly successful stock market investor wonders whether he could further improve his batting average.

In each of these cases, more distinct data are needed on the assumptions that underlie choices. These assumptions guide the person's response to a set of choices among which he must pick.

They thus determine the kinds of new information which will cause him to perceive a change in the nature of each available choice. Let us refer to each different kind of such information as gauging some attribute of the choice alternative.

For example, the young man needs more concrete detail on the special attributes guiding the interests of those he finds most attractive. He also needs to know where he stands in their eyes with respect to these attributes. The Detroit auto designer and the major political party have similar needs. Then, too, the intelligence expert needs to know what attributes are really used by policy-makers in making their decisions, and whether his reports describe anything along these attribute dimensions.

For a slightly different reason the head of the large government program and the manager with the new assistant also would like to know more about the assumptions guiding the actions of those to whom they are going to give power and money.

In the other two cases, the person making choices needs to know more about himself. Both the psychiatrist and the stock market investor need to see more clearly the concrete components on which their decisions are based before they try to go about improving their choices. They have reached the limits of their intuitive skill. Unconscious learning processes will carry them no further.

These plights have as a central thread the need to recognize the reasons why people make some choices rather than others.

Much of the theory in the social sciences and in psychology reflects the practical problem our cases suggest. Relevant basic research is being carried out in cognitive and social psychology and in management science. This book presents some of these results.

The methods developed here may have widespread use in building social theory because the problem they analyze is a central issue in microeconomics, in political science, in organization theory, and in the sociology of knowledge.

In a really basic sense, progress toward the solution of this problem is a key to applied management science. That is, in order to apply management science one usually has to understand the assumptions guiding the manager. It is in that context that my approach to the problem has been developed.

## 1.1. Purpose, Scope, and Plan

The central purpose of this book is to illustrate a method for finding out why people make some choices rather than others. This method will be referred to as measuring assumptions. When the interested reader has finished reading the book, he will be able to use this method to solve problems in his own field. In addition, he will have seen the details of likely uses in a management context.

The method was refined and tested in a study of stock market participants. Thus, the reader will get a rich view of the startling diversity in the attributes investors seem to use in picking stocks.

The account of the method and its test presume a basic knowledge of statistics. Broad familiarity with the social sciences is helpful but not essential.

The plan of the book follows this order. First, the problem to be solved is detailed in terms of managerial needs. Alternative possible measurement approaches and theories are described as they arise logically. An outline of the method for measuring assumptions is followed by the account of its use in a study of stock market participants. This narrative provides a practical handbook for the reader's use. A number of sample applications are shown in some detail. The final chapters speculate on uses of the method which are as yet untried.

## 1.2. The Problem in a Managerial Context

The process of making choices will be termed decision-making. We are all engaged full time at it. This decision-making, though, is mostly routine habit. Further, most choices put only small amounts of resources at risk. On the other hand, those people engaged in managing the affairs of large organizations must make choices that may commit large resources. Their choices are complex and often contain some novel or unstructured factors. Management scientists have found that the assumptions that guide managerial decisions are usually only partly conscious. Therefore, direct questioning of the manager is of limited usefulness. Also, adequately observing the manager as he makes the decisions in real time is often an extraordinarily time-consuming and expensive proposition. Thus, measuring managerial assumptions efficiently is a real and fruitful challenge for any solution to our problems.

Through the years, the skill of managerial decision-making has been raised to a fairly high level. It is well advanced in business firms faced with varied competitive forces over a long time span.

This evolution of improved decision-making in the firm has been slow, but clear. For example, the concept of money-measured profit helps keep decisions focused on a single goal. Double-entry bookkeeping and standard cost accounting help in making clear the variables needing attention in pursuit of profit. Formal budgets record and transmit some managerial assumptions about the means to this end. In the last few decades, further progress has been made in some cases through mathematical models of problem situations. Finally, the more recent use of the computer has been important in supporting all these aids to decision-making.

All these gains depend on increased explicitness. Assumptions have slowly become more clearly made, recorded, and explained. Our purpose is to increase yet further this explicitness. Let us try to construct a picture or scenario of what such further gains in explicitness might imply.

In this picture the manager more clearly records his goals and assumptions for types of decisions which are especially important. He is familiar with methods useful for getting this kind of explicitness in an easy way. Thus, he can obtain a record of his decision which he can compare through time with his changing assumptions as the decision outcome has its effect. He uses this record as a reminder of his plan. He also uses it as a guide to obtaining new knowledge arising from the difference between assumed and actual outcomes. The more detailed and concrete the record, the more he can use these differences to pinpoint the cause of his errors. As a result, he can better generalize what he learns to other choices involving similar assumptions.

The manager controls his own private record of assumptions. He selects certain task-related portions for communication and for access by other managers. Thus, some of the knowledge that he acquires is made permanently available for training purposes or for the use of others with like problems. Then too, this record allows improved coordination when more than one manager is working on the same large problem.

Also, as a result of clearer assumptions, routine organizational information systems are made more effective. Experts in designing such systems are better able to match information they can supply with that really likely to be used by the manager. Finding the lack of such a match is useful not only in system redesign but in teaching the manager to use the system well.

The foregoing scenario has not yet been realized. Nor is it a forced prediction. Unfortunately, managers, like most of us, do not yet know how to make themselves very explicit.

This phenomenon is well known to those who ask managers how they come to select particular courses of action or choice alternatives. One usually finds that the answers are not put in concrete, operational terms. Sometimes the answers are concrete but would not, in fact, have led to the decision patterns observed. Self-knowledge is both hard to transmit and often in error.

A major aim of the research presented in this book is to make some progress toward realizing our scenario.

To appreciate what kind of impact on managers such progress might have, contrast our scenario with present-day management accounting. The information available from the accounting system is moderately explicit but at the severe cost of confinement to financial transactions data. Though useful, it thus gives a narrow and partial view of problem situations. In general, decision processes may put to use information concerning a much broader scope of attributes. Such information includes attributes in the psychological, political, and technical realms. At present, these attributes are usually added to the decision in a haphazard and unrecorded manner.

Further, there is now little heed given to the needs of managers for their own individualized information. Designers of information systems to support routine decisions have begun to realize that managers in different jobs might usefully get different information. Yet, there is little recognition of the individual's special assumptions as a basis of information needs; thus differences in training, work experiences, and even temperament are usually ignored.

These current limits on information system relevance to the manager are to some extent balanced by benefits in terms of objectivity and feasibility. The argument often given against change in directions such as those suggested in this book is that the results would be too subjective and cost too much.

The present research does not accept today's information systems as dogma. It seeks to show benefits of extending explicitness beyond these traditional bounds into the realm of subjective decision assumptions. That is, subjective assumptions made explicit in a practical manner will be indicated as useful inputs to managerial information systems.

This development is in accord with the characteristic evolution of knowledge in all fields. Characteristically, the qualitative and personal subjective models of a few people become slowly crystallized into quantitative, objectified models, widely known by many. Better methods of measuring assumptions may well speed up that process in management science.

## In Summary
Problems of discovering why decision-makers choose the specific alternatives they do are very general and of deep practical importance. However, naïve questioning is often ineffective. Successful empathy remains an intuitive art. What seems to be needed are reproducible methods that yield useful models of decision assumptions without requiring impractical amounts of effort.

The field of management offers promising application for such methods because the resources committed there by repetitive decisions are often large. Also, we have before us a history of

advances in explicitness in management which have been extremely successful, such as standard cost accounting. Therefore, in our
aim for better measures of decision assumptions, we shall be
heuristically guided by the need to find a satisfactory method for
management use.

# 2

A Model of Decision-Making
and Its Measurement

Before trying to measure decision assumptions, we need a model of decision-making which gives operational meaning to our concept. This short chapter discusses the model of decision-making and assumptions used in this book. It also introduces the problem of estimating relationships within the model from real-life decision-makers.

## 2.1. Assumptions, Decision Nets, and Their Representation

A theme that we shall pursue is the sequential, partly repetitive, nature of decision-making. All decisions to which we can apply some knowledge must have something in common with other decisions made in the past. It is basically by observing the outcomes of past decisions that we obtain the knowledge to make present decisions with some intelligence. This "knowledge," which may be only partly valid, is what I mean by an assumption. The reader is asked to suspend his intuition on this point and simply to view assumptions as a network of causal relationships linking goals and the perceived situation to consequent decisions.

Consider a thermostat controlling a room heater. When perceived temperature gets too much colder than some desired temperature, an electric switch is closed. Closing the switch is the decision. What is the assumption? The assumption, which was inserted by the designer, is that closing the switch will result in an *increase* in temperature rather than its decrease, thus solving the problem of a too-cold room.

Decisions made by humans are a good deal more complicated. The causal relationships linking perceptions to action may be branched and intricately interwoven. Still, their pattern always embodies a set of assumptions about the world's response to our actions. Thus, it may be fruitful to model these assumptions in

terms of such causal relationships. That is, assumptions will be
viewed in the most general way by thinking of the information
processing or decision-making causal nets in which they are
embodied.

Let's look at a simplified constructed example. The head of a
family must choose a house in a new city to which he has been
transferred for two years. We shall assume that he has only one
week in which to decide and is unfamiliar with what is available.
This decision process is shown in Figure 2.1. The network of
causal relations illustrated there will be referred to as a decision
net.

As constructed here, this is a fairly simple decision, but it illus-
trates several features that would make the assumptions within it
difficult to measure in real-world situations.

For example, the decision net in Figure 2.1 does not in general
cause all available alternative houses to be considered. Once an
acceptable house is found, search stops. This makes empirical
measurement of assumptions more difficult because only those
alternatives actually considered give us meaningful observations.

Models of decision processes which allow search to stop and the
choice to be made before all alternatives within a specified choice
set are considered are termed "satisficing" models.[1] Those that
require all members of a prespecified choice set to be considered
and the best one chosen according to some criterion are termed
"optimizing" models.

Often we identify the decision itself with our model of it. Thus,
we speak of optimizing or satisficing decisions. Figure 2.1 is a

1. Choice set is used here to mean the set of alternatives before choice. Some
authors have used it to mean the set of most preferred alternatives after
choice.

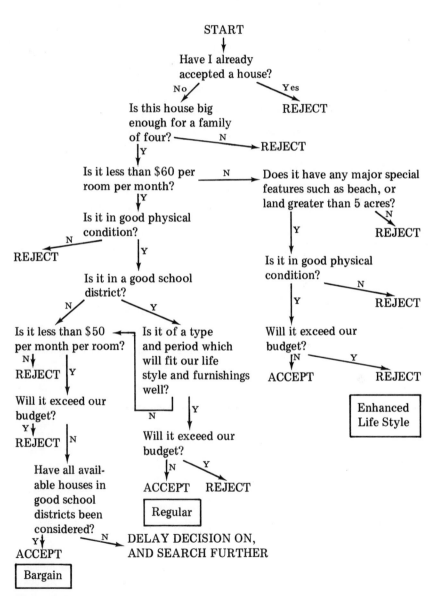

Figure 2.1
A Decision Net for House Purchases

satisficing model. There is no criterion function associated with it simpler than the decision net itself.

If we wanted a model of optimizing behavior, and this is the sort about which economists have written much, we might obtain it through a different decision net, as indicated in Figure 2.2. This network forces all the alternatives to be considered, at least within the relevant domain. Note, however, that in the real world there is always some constraint that keeps the number of alternatives actually considered within some bounds. This bounded set we shall call the choice set. Note also that even in this example the choice set includes the alternative of choosing no house.

In our example, any decision net corresponding to an optimizing decision would probably involve the direct comparison of two houses at a time. Or perhaps it might involve comparing each alternative house to some quantitative reference yardstick. In either case, all the alternatives would be considered, and at least in the second case a complete ordering of all the alternative houses would be obtained.[2] Then we could represent the decision either by a decision net or by an ordering on the set of alternatives. In the latter, the budget constraint would establish the attainable set within the choice set. The alternative selected would be the most preferred member within the attainable set according to a criterion function to be optimized. To show how this surface behavior might arise from an underlying decision net, we shall include some further memory facilities in the decision net and also another outcome — provisional acceptance pending further information

2. It is, of course possible to obtain a complete ordering by multiple pairwise comparisons. Sometimes, also, decision processes may consider all the available alternatives without completely ordering them.

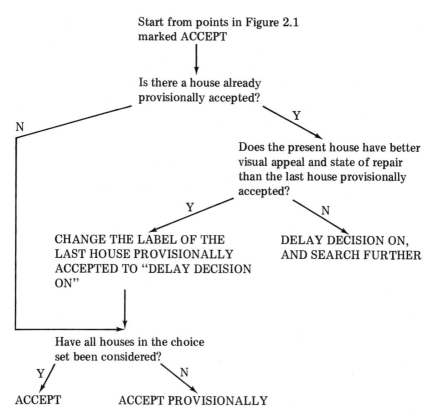

Figure 2.2
A Fragment of an Optimizing Decision. Note: Depending on the location in the decision net of Figure 2.1, the choice set is meant to include one of the following three sets: "regular," "bargain," or "enhanced life style" housing.

processing. These features of the decision net are shown in Figure 2.2.

Decision nets such as the one in Figure 2.2 may be modeled to any degree of precision through a choice-set representation. That is, since for optimization all alternatives within a set are considered, we can represent the characteristics of the decision process in terms of a graph linking the attribute characteristics of the set of alternatives to the decision outcomes.[3] Only those attributes bearing on the constraints or the criterion to be optimized need be considered in this representation of the decision alternatives. This is not true of decision nets such as the one shown in Figure 2.1.

In all cases, however, we can represent a decision directly through a decision net that takes into account the process involved. Figures 2.1 and 2.2 are both decision-net representations.

To repeat, however, if the decision process to be modeled does not force all the alternatives in the choice set to be considered then a representation of the choice set alone does not allow a precise explanation of the decisions made. In this case, attributes that influence the *sequence* of alternatives considered influence the final decision. Here, precise explanations depend on a direct model of the decision net. A choice-set representation gives only an approximation, at best, of the result of the decision process.

Usually, the outcomes of optimizing decision processes are conveniently modeled by familiar mathematical representations of orderings within the alternative choice set. Thus, perhaps, the portion of our house-buyer's decision process within an optimization fragment of his decision net shown in Figure 2.2 might be

3. Here "graph" is used in the mathematical sense. See Bourbaki (1968).

modeled something like this:

Absolute house preference $= a_0 + a_1 V + a_2 R,$

where $V$ is a measure of visual attractiveness and $R$ is a measure of repair work needed. The statistical procedures for empirically deriving a model using such choice-set representations, particularly the simple linear ones, are well developed. Modeling decision nets directly, that is, the decision process, is a much more difficult and relatively unexplored art.

Whether or not the decision net represents an optimizing or a satisficing decision, there are other difficulties in measuring it. Note that in our example the branches of the net most traversed in practice depend on the types of house available and the budget size. Any measures relying on observation of the net in its use would tend to discover first those portions of the decision net used most often. Unless we keep the used portions relatively constant from observation sample to observation sample, it is very difficult to discover, in general, the exact assumption relationships in the net. Suppose the budget is low. In the case that we have considered, only "bargain" housing will be accepted. In the bargain case, attributes of price and good physical condition have an influence, but the type of school district and major special features have no independent influence on the house finally chosen. If the budget is somewhat higher, any of the three types, enhanced life style, regular, or bargain, might be bought. Thus the attribute of price per room per month has less and less direct influence as the budget goes up. The environment also influences the choices available. Consider the effect of the school district constraint. In our decision net, if all the housing available passes this criterion, there is no way to observe this test in action.

Suppose a diverse available choice set is held relatively constant from observation to observation. Now we have a better chance to measure decision assumptions. There are, we shall see, a variety of measuring methods one might use. Each is appropriate and practical for discovering certain features of the decision net in all its generality. We have already implied that some means might better measure optimizing decision nets than satisficing decision nets.

## 2.2. Measuring Decision Assumptions with Naïve Least-Squares Regression

The average social scientist, in trying to predict human decisions, finds himself trying to apply multivariate least-squares regression or its close relative, the analysis of variance. These are probably the best developed empirical modeling techniques. Usually he first hypothesizes a simple linear relationship. What kind of underlying decision net corresponds to this particular choice-set representation? This approach really implies that the decision-maker can order the alternatives in a metric fashion, such that his preference $Y$ is expressible as a cardinal number. If, however, the observable $Y$ is not cardinal, for example if we cannot get any ordering information on the preference for the alternatives except the decision results *accept*, *reject*, or *delay decision on*, regression or analysis of variance procedures often gives us results that are hard to interpret. In this case, we need to use multiway discriminant analysis to get at the assumption relationships.

Even when this assumption of a cardinal preference is valid, the linear hypothesis restricts the range of assumptions one can correctly discover. Let us suppose that the same assumptions relating attributes to preference hold no matter what the level of preference. Let the various tests or questions be dummy variables, $X_i$,

$i = 1, \ldots, n$, where $n$ is the number of different test attributes or questions. If we run the attribute and preference data of each alternative in the choice set actually considered through a linear multiple regression algorithm we obtain an equation:

$$Y = a_0 + a_1 X_1 + a_2 X_2 + \ldots + a_n X_n.$$

Can we then use this equation to predict perfectly from attribute data preferences among these alternatives? In general, no. This equation will be only a linear approximation of a nonlinear function.

The possibility of nonlinearity of the function with respect to a single attribute is only a minor problem However, the dependence of the function on a nonlinear *combination* of different attributes may be a serious obstacle to empirical modeling of the decision process or of the decision assumptions. Since the number of possible nonlinear combining functions is too large to search exhaustively, usually the most practical approach is to first model the process linearly and then to explain portions of the error through one or more interaction effects among the attributes. However, since the number of different interaction possibilities goes up nearly exponentially with the number of different attributes which are branch points in the decision net, this still may be a difficult or impossible task. In addition, rooting out and curing the standard regression problems under these conditions may require infeasible amounts of observations.[4]

A still further serious problem is that in trying to measure the

4. These standard obstacles to use of the regression model are heteroscedasticity, autocorrelation, multicollinearity among the tests or attributes, inappropriate distribution of the error term (normality is the most favorable), and errors in attribute measures. See Johnston (1963) for a review of procedures for discovering and coping with these problems.

decision assumptions we may not even accurately know the attribute test used. On the one hand, we may not know all of the
attributes used in the decision net. On the other hand, we may
"know" some that are not really used. When we leave out used
attributes or put in spurious attributes, we tend to create further
serious errors in our regression models of the decision assumptions.

Fortunately, many real-world decisions nets seem to be
moderately approximatable by a linear regression of preference
against an attribute representation of the choice set. That is, a
number of experimental tests have shown that naïve linear regression models do a fairly good job of summarizing the assumptions in some decisions.[5] Thus, despite all its problems, linear
regression is often the best, simplest, and most feasible starting
point for modeling decision assumptions through a choice-set
representation. If this fails, it may be necessary to model directly
the decision net through a detailed examination of the decision
process while it is at work.

In reality, most human decisions are not fully optimizing, nor
are they linear. The role of the linear equation relating attributes
to preferences is thus almost always one of efficiently summarizing the easiest aspect of assumptions to model. This role leads one
to conjecture why such a substantial part of human decisions can
often be captured through such naïve models. If assumptions
reflect what decision-makers have learned about the world, perhaps assumptions are so largely linearly approximatable precisely
because linear models have the greatest ratio of useful return to
learning effort for the decision-maker himself.

5. See Slovic (1969).

**In Summary**

To make the notion of "decision assumption" as operational as practicable, we view it in the context of a decision net, as in Figure 2.1. In general, measuring assumptions may be viewed as discovering the causal structure of the decision net. This requires observing the decision process step by step. However, some types of optimizing decisions can be modeled without reference to the process of decision-making. This is done through representation of the results of the process in ordering the set of alternatives, the choice set. In this case, measuring decision assumptions means discovering the attributes which are associated with alternatives achieving a preferred rank in the ordering and measuring their relative influence.

The simplest approach to the latter is multivariate regression. However, there are many hazards, including lack of cardinality, multicollinearity among the attributes, and misspecification of the relevant attributes. When regression is applied to the results of nonoptimizing decisions, other problems appear and those above are magnified.

# 3

How might one go about better modeling decision assumptions? What is the state of this art and of relevant scientific knowledge?

This chapter draws together some of the threads of social science which can contribute to our understanding of what is involved in the measurement of decision assumptions. Its aim is twofold. The first is to bring us to a feasible and effective measurement methodology. The second, equally important, is to make possible a greater awareness of the implications of advances in measurement methodology for the further development of social science.

This scientific work is discussed in three broad categories: normative choice-set representations, descriptive choice-set representations, and models of information processing or decision nets.

## 3.1. Normative Choice-Set Representations

The most popular models of decision-making in the social sciences are those of microeconomics. The theory of microeconomics is constructed on axioms that imply a choice-set representation of decision-making. Decision alternatives that satisfy the constraints, if any, on the decision outcome are labeled the available choice set. Within the available choice set there are one or more subsets, called indifference sets, which are mutually exclusive and exhaustive. The axioms assume the decision-maker can completely rank order his preferences for the indifference sets. He is assumed to be indifferent among alternatives within any single indifference set. That is, the decision-maker is willing to select randomly the particular alternative chosen from an indifference set. His final choice is restricted to the indifference set that is most preferred among all those within the available choice set.

This model is presumed wherever microeconomics is applied. It appears innocuous, indeed, almost a tautology. This appearance can be deceptive. The class of decision processes which the micro-economic model is capable of modeling precisely is restricted, as we saw in the previous chapter. It is restricted to those processes that force all available alternatives to be considered, and further restricted to those that establish a complete ordering of alternatives.[1]

There is a third major restriction. Microeconomics goes further and asserts that if the constraints on the available choice set are changed, this will not change the preference ordering of the alternatives already considered. The notion that empirically measured preferences are transitive is intimately related to this fixity. Thereby microeconomics rules out precise modeling of a broad class of decision nets which do force all available alternatives to be considered but where the information processing strategy implies changes in assumptions as the number or type of available alternatives changes. Many cognitive processing limitations on choice, such as memory limits or time deadlines, are thus not representable within the microeconomic model.

There is ample evidence that many real-world decision processes are thereby eliminated from precise descriptive consideration. Equally serious, prescriptive implications in a world of necessary cognitive limitations are thus placed in fundamental jeopardy.

Microeconomic models are thus merely descriptive approximations. They do become precise, however, if we choose to regard them as ideals, or norms, rather than descriptions. Economists speak of decision processes that deviate from such choice-set

1. Of course, the further question of whether the alternatives form a completely ordered set also presumes that they are all considered. See Von Neumann and Morgenstern (1947).

representations as "irrational." It is important to realize that this does not imply, at least to this writer, that decision procedures that are "irrational" in this sense may not be more feasible and useful in some cases than those that would be labeled "rational."

There is a fourth restriction of the types of decision nets which can be modeled precisely by microeconomics. In most micro-economic model applications the axioms are further extended so that the choice set may be represented as a Euclidean space of $n$ dimensions. Each of these dimensions corresponds to some attri-bute along which each alternative takes a value. The preference ordering over alternatives in this space is axiomatically presumed to be such that some regions of neighboring points in the space are more preferred than others. For example this space may be axio-matized as *connected.* Thereby lexicographic preference orderings are made unrepresentable.[2]

A fifth major restriction is that the more preferred regions are axiomatized to have mathematical properties of not only connec-tedness, but also convexity. Roughly speaking, in a convex set, all points on a straight line connecting any two points in the set are also in the set. The convexity property rules out precise modeling of another wide class of decision nets. For example, one can imagine useful decision nets where above a certain threshold in some primary attribute the alternative is judged preferable if it has *more* of some secondary attribute, while below that threshold in primary attribute an alternative is judged preferable the *less* it has

2. Connectedness is a technical term regarding the topological properties of the space. Connectedness underlies the condition that arbitrarily close alter-natives will be arbitrarily similarly preferred. See Debreu (1954) and George-scu-Roegen (1954). A lexicographic ordering is one in which certain subor-dinate attributes influence the choice only if there is a "tie" within some difference threshold regarding a more important attribute. Psychological thresholds imply lexicographic ordering.

of the secondary attribute. All such decision nets are ruled out by the microeconomic notion of a choice space in which the more preferred alternatives are members of convex regions.

In limited regions of such microeconomic choice spaces, the preference of one alternative over another may be predictable as a fairly simple function of the alternatives' coordinates in the attribute space. For example, we may have, in an attribute space of $n$ dimensions, some region where alternative $A$ is preferred to $B$ if and only if the function $a_1 X_{1A} + a_2 X_{2A} + \ldots + a_n X_{nA}$ is greater than $a_1 X_{1B} + a_2 X_{2B} + \ldots + a_n X_{nB}$, where $X$ is an attribute position.

Economists call the value of such a function for alternative $A$ the *utility* of alternative $A$. When one reads in economic literature of attempts to measure utility as a function of various attributes, there is always underlying some implicit decision that is being measured, sometimes unwittingly. In this sense, such utility measures are a type of what are in this book labeled as measures of decision assumptions.

Historically, there has been a good deal of difficulty in reconciling the economist's specialized choice-set representation with decision processes in which the decision-maker must deal with uncertainty or risk. An important contribution by Von Neumann and Morgenstern, later extended by Savage, was to show how one might plausibly map both certain and risky alternatives into the same attribute space, using the decision-maker's own subjective probabilities and risk preferences.[3]

3. Of course, much more widely appreciated is their accompanying demonstration that in this space a cardinal utility function could be used to predict preferences for risky events. This scheme axiomatizes a complete preference ordering, and thus an underlying optimizing decision net. It also presumes the other restrictions mentioned for microeconomics. See Von Neumann and Morgenstern (1947).

Two comments are in order. The first deals generally with comparisons between uncertain alternatives. The second deals with comparisons between certain and uncertain alternatives.

First, these axiomatizations impose all the restrictions implicit in the microeconomic model of choice. That is, we suppose consideration of all the alternatives, complete ordering, irrelevance of constraints on the available choice set in determining the preference ordering, and that the preference regions be connected and convex. Now such axioms become less plausible as descriptive models as the environment becomes more uncertain. In relatively unexplored choice sets, many of the alternatives must be effortfully generated, thus preventing consideration of "all" of the alternatives. Inexperience in making tradeoffs between attributes in certain regions of the attribute space in which the alternatives are embedded makes implausible complete preference ordering. Sequential learning while processing the alternatives makes preference ordering depend on availability constraints. Errors in observation necessitate psychological thresholds and make lexicographic ordering more predominant. Gaps in experience with the full choice set tends to cause decision processes to follow different attributes and regimes in the separate well-known regions, thus destroying convexity. Therefore, extreme uncertainty poses a threat to *each* of the major axioms of microeconomics.

Second, the placement by von Neumann and Morgenstern, and others, of certain alternatives within the space of uncertain alternatives is axiomatized in the same way. In order to give the preference regions convenient topological properties, they have supposed monotonicity. That is, the condition that a certain alternative $p$ is preferred to another certain alternative $q$ must imply that any lottery of $p$ and $q$ is preferred to $q$. However, this

is in general true only if there are no externality effects. I argue
that in the real world of limited cognitive ability and hierarchical
decision trees, one is *always* dealing with local subdecisions existing in parallel with other complementary local subdecisions. Even
though cognitive ability is too limited to optimize the local decisions globally, one may often be able to partly characterize the
interdependencies between them. Whether or not the monotonicity
condition holds for a local subdecision depends on the decision-maker's vague perception of these interdependencies or com-
plementarities. To put it simply, one may justifiably be "irration-
ally" risk averse with regard to a local decision if one suspects the
need for coordination with another parallel local decision. One
may well look for this circumstance when statistical decision
theorists fail to obtain so-called consistent subjective probability
and utility estimates from real-world decision-makers.[4]

One hope for improved prescriptive models of decision processes lies in the understanding gained through improved description. Our empirical measurement of decision assumptions may lay
a foundation for future progress in this direction.

## Systems Analysis

A kind of applied microeconomics in management which has become popular in the last two decades is variously known as program planning and budgeting or sometimes as "system analysis."
This approach carries the same strengths and weaknesses as microeconomics. The work of E. S. Quade and various analysts at the
Rand Corporation over this period contains many good examples
of the approach. At its best, this consists of a reasonably orderly
procedure for helping make a decision; the procedure elicits much
of the kind of explicitness in assumptions sought through the

4. See Friedman and Savage (1948).

present research. Managers are encouraged to reach new levels of explicitness by participating in the construction and operation of a simplified "model" of the real situation (see Quade 1967). This model is then embedded in a microeconomic choice framework. Thus, associated with this model are the decision-maker's objectives, estimates of the result and cost attributes for each alternative, and a criterion that can be used to get a complete preference ordering of the alternatives. In practice, this criterion has implied the Euclidean space choice-set representation. In addition, according to Quade, effective systems analysis follows an iterative procedure through the following cycle in support of the decision: formulating the problem, selecting the criterion, designing better alternatives, collecting data, building new models, evaluating the alternatives, testing for the sensitivity of the preference ordering to changes in the estimates of alternative characteristics, questioning these estimates, reexamining the objectives, and so on, until satisfaction or time or money pressure forces a cutoff.

In my opinion, the specification of this procedure and the emphasis on an explicit, easily communicable model underlying the decision are the most valuable contributions of systems analysis. The attempt to force the decision process to conform to one that is susceptible to a microeconomic choice-set representation probably does more good than harm, on average, but is sometimes distracting.

On the other hand, the weaknesses of systems analysis are readily apparent to practicing managers who attempt to use the method as it is presently practiced. Very often in uncertain managerial situations, the objectives and the attributes that measure progress toward them are multiple and the tradeoffs not readily quantifiable. This leads to difficulty in constructing the Euclidean space choice representation. Second, the decision-maker's assumptions are often obscure, even to himself. Practicing systems analysts have demonstrated rather modest skill in eliciting them. This manifests itself not only in decision models that imprecisely weight attributes but also in models that entirely omit important attributes that the systems analyst has missed.

### 3.2. Descriptive Choice-Set Representations

Choice-set representations of decisions processes need not be normative, nor derived from abstract theory. Suppose one measures the alternatives in the available choice set along some relevant attributes and also obtains the decision-maker's preferences among these alternatives. The conjunction of these two types of data may provide a highly useful model of the decision process and its assumptions. In contrast to a normative view, one need not feel chagrin when the descriptive model proves an imperfect predictor of further decisions from the same process. Indeed, an error term is often made explicit, since such descriptions are usually statistical in origin. The test is not whether the derived prediction is perfect, but whether it is useful.

Such descriptive choice-set representations may be combined with the following kinds of preference information, in order of increasing mathematical strength:
1. partial ordering among alternatives,
2. complete preference ordering among alternatives,
3. quantitative measures of preference.

In this exposition we confine ourselves to a treatment of methods using the third type, quantitative preference data. The reader should note, however, that the methods to be described have their weaker analogues.

A good deal of the work done by econometricians may be characterized as descriptive choice-set representation. By and large, econometricians have been unsuccessful in predicting individual decision-maker behavior. They thus usually confine themselves to aggregated data reflecting large numbers of individuals. A reasonable conjecture might be made that the economists' relative difficulty in predicting individual behavior stems from two influences. These are, first, their lack of sensitivity in eliciting the attributes used by individuals in characterizing alternatives, and second, the benefits of aggregation in reducing the apparent "irrationality" induced by their choice-set representation.

There has been much work in the last forty years in the areas of attitude and opinion research characterizable as descriptive choice-set representation. More recently, market research and cognitively oriented psychology have endeavored to describe decisions in these terms. In the process, special measurement techniques have been developed for modeling decision assumptions which go beyond the techniques of standard econometrics.

The resulting art of modeling through descriptive choice-set representation is much better developed than that of direct modeling of decision nets. There appear to be two chief reasons for this. First, normative models of decision have thus far been framed in terms of choice-set representations. Second, empirical estimation requires observations. It is much easier to observe the input and final output of a decision process in terms of the attributes of the alternatives than to observe the intermediate information processes at work.

In this section, we review some existing methods of descriptively measuring assumptions within the choice-set representation framework. In order to better understand their respective advantages and limitations, let us focus our attention on a very simple situation — a preference as a real-valued function of a single attribute variable in a choice-set representation.

One may describe such simple assumptions in terms of the following three elements for each alternative in the available choice set: an alternative's position on a preference scale; an alternative's position on an attribute scale; and a relation between them.

Let us shift the context of decision-making from the house-buyer of Chapter 2 to the scene of most of the examples to be given in the remainder of the book, the stock market. Suppose we wish to measure the assumptions of different decision-makers regarding the desirability of XYZ Corporation's common stock. They may differ in three distinct ways:

1. in the position of XYZ Corporation along a particular attribute used in common by several decision-makers;

2. in the attributes used by the decision-makers to characterize XYZ Corporation.

3. in the relation linking the attribute to the decision-maker's desire for the stock.

For example, one decision-maker might assume that a recent increase in XYZ Corporation's marketing capability resulted in a favorable change in the desirability of its stock, while the second decision-maker might assume that a recent decrease in XYZ's marketing capability resulted in an unfavorable change in the desirability of its stock. Over the choice set, their assumptions are the same: that recent increases of a firm's marketing capability result in a more desirable stock, and vice versa. At the level of this particular alternative, they differ because they ascribe different positions of XYZ Corporation on the attribute, "recent changes in marketing capability."

A third decision-maker differs from each of these. He assumes a different relation. That is, he assumes a recent increase in XYZ Corporation's marketing ability has resulted in a *decrease* in the desirability of its stock.[5]

Consider, in contrast, the difference between these assumptions and one by a fourth decision-maker, that recent sharp increases in the price of XYZ's stock have resulted in a favorable change in its desirability. Here the attribute used to characterize XYZ's situation, recent price changes, is along a dimension entirely different from that employed by the other decision-makers. Thus, if we want to explain differences in choices made among these decision-makers, it is important to measure the attribute dimension used to characterize an alternative as well as the alternative's position on the dimension.

**Measurement Procedures**

How can one measure the attribute dimensions — that is, discover the relevant attributes? This is a key issue in choice-set representation. One obvious method is direct questioning of the decision-maker. However, this approach is of limited usefulness because we often cannot rely on the decision-maker to give an accurate assessment of his own, perhaps partly unconscious, assumptions. This inaccuracy occurs even when the decision-maker himself is asking the questions. When an outside observer asks the questions, the observer's preconceptions and biases limit reliability further.

Another reasonable approach to discovering the relevant attributes is for an outside observer to prespecify a large list of potentially relevant input attributes. He may then use observation and regression analysis of the preferences against the attribute values

5. Less drastically, he might presume a relation of different strength, rather than one of opposite direction.

to narrow the list. However, for really individualized subjective assumptions this is inefficient at best and often misses the point entirely.[6]

More sophisticated methods which are particularly oriented toward discovering pertinent attributes are the semantic differential, the various multidimensional scaling methods (MDS), and the role repertory test. These are now described.[7]

*The Semantic Differential and Factor Analysis*

In order to explain the semantic differential it may be fruitful to describe briefly factor analysis. For a mathematical, as opposed to intuitive, treatment, see Harman (1967), or Anderson (1958).

Suppose one has characterized a set of objects along three attributes, $x$, $y$, and $z$. The object of factor analysis is to discover any new attributes linearly derivable from combinations of $x$, $y$, and $z$ which more efficiently describe these objects. What does it mean to describe efficiently? Very broadly speaking, it means that distinctions among the objects can be expressed in terms of as few as possible attributes.

The method that maximizes this criterion is known as principal components analysis. Other methods widely known as factor analysis subscribe to the goal of efficient description but make some compromises to attain another goal, which may be broadly labeled simple factor structure. In an intuitive sense, simple factor structure implies that the mapping from original attributes to the

6. See Slovic (1969) for the analysis of variance approach on a similar problem. An additional insidious problem of these methods is the observer's tendency to project his own perceived attribute values rather than the subject's perceived attribute values into the analysis.

7. See Osgood, Suci, and Tannenbaum (1957) for a description of the semantic differential and Harman (1967) for a review of factor analysis. See Silk (1969) for a relatively recent discussion of multidimensional scaling. See Bieri (1955) for an account of Kelly's role repertory test.

newly constructed attributes, along which more efficient description is possible, be of a simple form. Such methods generally
produce new attributes termed *factors* or *attribute factors*. These
are aggregations of only a few of the attributes, and *vice versa.*

These notions are illustrated in Figure 3.1. Suppose we represent twenty objects as being in a three-dimensional box whose
edges are axes parallel to the $x$, $y$, and $z$ attributes. Each dot in the
box represents one of these objects.

Suppose we were to intersect the box with a single line that had
the property that it was closest in a least-squares sense to the dots
and that it lay very close to the line $db$ in the figure. Then a newly
defined attribute factor approximately parallel to $db$ would be the
first principal component, $F_1$, in this situation. This factor, however, is not sufficient to describe all distinctions among the objects

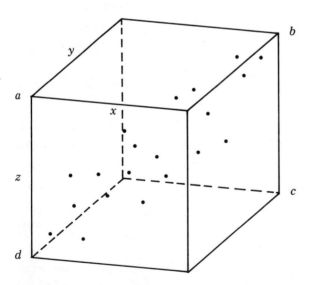

Figure 3.1
Twenty Objects Described by Attributes $x$, $y$, and $z$

in the box. Suppose we intersect the box with a plane including the line $F_1$, where the plane again has the property that it is the plane nearest the twenty dots. In the figure suppose this plane is defined by $abcd$ in the figure. Then the second principal component, $F_2$, is the line at right angles to $db$ lying in that plane.

The remaining small amount of variation in the box could be described by the axis at right angles to this plane. This axis is $F_3$. Most of the distinctions among the objects can now be described in terms of $F_1$, or sometimes $F_1$ and $F_2$, rather than using all three original attributes, $x$, $y$, and $z$. Thus, a more efficient description has been obtained.

In order to obtain a simpler structure, the three new axes $F_1$, $F_2$, and $F_3$ might be *rotated* so that they were in a simpler relation to the original attributes. For example, we might get new factors $G_1$ and $G_2$ within the plane $abcd$ such that $G_1$ was at right angles to $z$ and $G_2$ was parallel to it. In this case, the two factors would still together do the work of $F_1$ and $F_2$ but would be easier to interpret and measure.

With this understanding of factor analysis, the reader is in a better position to appreciate the nature of the semantic differential. In brief, the semantic differential is based on a factor analysis of multiple decision-makers' ratings of objects on a large number of more or less relevant prespecified adjective scales. These objects can then be automatically rated on the summarizing attribute factors, if any, revealed by the factor analysis. Usually, the factor analysis is based on ratings by all the decision-makers on all the scales. A comparison of the factor scores of the objects to the individual's preferences then gives a measure of each individual's assumptions relating the factor attributes to his preferences.

This use of the semantic differential combined with regression is more efficient than straightforward regression against the original attributes. Because it first reduces the attributes to a smaller number of factors before trying to relate them to preferences, the regression estimation can locate pertinent attributes with less statistical error. However, the semantic differential faces several important problems. First, combining the decision-makers' ratings before factor analysis obscures, rather than elicits, individual differences in attributes used in their decision nets. Second, there is the difficulty in making the prespecified adjective scales sufficiently specific and relevant to the problem at hand. Third, the method of rating objects on a standard seven- or nine-point scale for every adjective makes rather strong assumptions about the metric nature of these scales.

If one performed a separate factor analysis for each decision-maker one could better get at differences between persons in the attribute structure used to characterize the same set of objects. However, this has not been done extensively because meaningful, statistically significant factors are hard to obtain with a reasonably small number of objects to be rated on a large number of partly irrelevant adjective scales. Aggregating the responses of a number of people reduces the statistical problem but obliterates individual differences. One thing clearly needed is a way of selecting more relevant adjective scales before the factor analysis.

*Multidimensional Scaling*

The second group of methods, multidimensional scaling (MDS), does not face the problems of the semantic differential. Multidimensional scaling methods use estimates or comparisons of interobject *similarities* to build up a spatial configuration of objects in which dissimilarities correspond to interobject distances. The resulting spatial configuration is supposed to correspond in some sense to the psychological configuration from which the similarity estimates were drawn by the decision-maker.

Until the past decade the input data required for MDS were a set of real, positive numbers specifying the interobject distances among all possible pairs of objects. These distances were analyzed to obtain a spatial configuration whose interobject distances satisfied to some degree of accuracy the initial specifications. More recently Shepard (1962) and others have discovered that if the number of objects was large relative to the number of dimensions, the original configuration could be approximately recovered with much weaker input data. In particular, it was only required to rank order the interobject distances or similarities of all the object pairs. The degree of approximation of the configuration obtained after analyzing these data to the original configuration from which the data were drawn is rather surprisingly good. It can be increased without limit by adding input data relating new objects to the others in the configuration. The only other requirement is that the number of dimensions of the configuration to be recovered be prespecified.

To see how this might work in a simple one-dimensional situation, consider Figures 3.2 and 3.3. Suppose we have three objects $A$, $B$, and $C$. Suppose their interobject distances or dissimilarities are ranked $AB \geqslant AC \geqslant BC$. Then in relation to the line defined by $AB$ we obtain a restriction on the permissible metric region for the line $AB$ in which $C$ may be located. This permissible region for

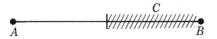

Figure 3.2
Permissible Region for $C$, where $AB \geqslant AC \geqslant BC$

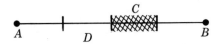

Figure 3.3
Permissible Region for $C$ where $AB \geqslant BD \geqslant AC \geqslant BC \geqslant AD \geqslant CD$

$C$ is crosshatched in Figure 3.2. Suppose now another object $D$ is also to be taken into account. Suppose the new rankings of distances be as follows: $AB \geqslant BD \geqslant AC \geqslant BC \geqslant AD \geqslant CD$. The new, smaller permissible region for $C$ in relation to $AB$ is double-crosshatched in Figure 3.3. As more new objects are taken into account, the permissible region for $C$, and for all the other objects, will decline further. We can approach a metric representation as closely as we wish. The same is true for larger numbers of dimensions although the calculation of the permissible region is laborious and infeasible without the aid of a computer.

Suppose, however, that there are four objects whose configuration could not be perfectly embedded in a one-dimensional space. One example would be where their distances are related as follows: $AB \geqslant CD \geqslant AD \geqslant CB \geqslant AC \geqslant DB$. This relationship is impossible for four distinct points in a one-dimensional space. For such input, MDS generates a one-dimensional configuration which has the least possible stress. Very roughly speaking, stress is analogous to the force that would have to be applied to some real-world configuration whose interobject spans were occupied by coil springs in order to compress the configuration to the required number of dimensions.

The particular initial configuration determines the minimum number of dimensions of the space in which it can be "easily" embedded. Multidimensional scaling provides a stress measure that gives the user a signal as to how many dimensions are required.

Criteria similar in role to those for factor analysis determine the axes of the most useful coordinate system in this space. Again, the resulting coordinates of objects can be associated with preferences to measure assumptions. In contrast to the semantic differential, no pre-specification of attributes is necessary and only weak ordinal assumptions as to the types of comparisons of similarity used by the decision-maker are required. These two important advantages make multidimensional scaling well suited for investigation of individual differences in attribute dimensions used to characterize objects.[8]

Studies using MDS have demonstrated important differences among decision-makers in the attribute dimensions they use to characterize a set of objects.[9] Such multidimensional scaling measures can be combined with measures on a known rating or preference scale to determine assumptions.[10]

For example, Cliff has related multidimensional scaling measures of the attribute structure used by students in describing fields of academic study to their ratings of likings for these fields. Rigney and De Bow similarly have related dimensions used by military officers to characterize simulations of attacks to their ratings of the degree of threat implicit in such attacks. Green and Maheshwari have used MDS to relate attributes used by business school

8. See Shepard (1962) and Kruskal (1964) for a description of the breakthrough that led to the new, powerful methods for multidimensional scaling which have been developed in the last decade. See Tucker and Messick (1963) for early work on individual differences.
9. See Horan (1969) and Warr, Schroder, and Blackman (1969) for recent studies regarding such individual differences.
10. See Cliff (1969), Rigney and De Bow (1967), and Green and Maheshwari (1969). See also Klahr (1969).

students to characterize business firms and their preference ratings of the firms' common stocks.

Though the technical feasibility of MDS for assumption measurement has thus been suggested, there appear to be remaining difficulties with MDS which the methodology to be described in the remainder of this book appears to overcome substantially.

Despite their elegance, multidimensional scaling methods seem relatively infeasible for moderately complicated practical situations. First, they require quite large numbers of similarity comparisons in order to construct a stable metric of adequate dimensions. Further, sometimes the decision-maker's task of combining similarities on various more or less independent attributes into a summary similarity response for pairs or triads of stimulus objects imposes additional work of deciding on combinatorial weights. Both factors increase the decision-maker's work load.

Another serious difficulty, that of interpreting the resulting dimensions, is aggravated because MDS discards available introspective data. That is, the labels of the attributes used in forming the summary similarity judgments are not elicited.

While this problem of misinterpretation of dimensions by an outside observer is not unique to MDS, its seriousness is usually much less in semantic differential or other factor analytic methods because one has available the loadings with fairly commonly understood semantic labels to support the factor dimension.

In many applications of decision assumptions measurement, for example in market research, one needs to be able to map the decision-maker's peculiar perceived dimensions into more common, or at least one's own, perceived attribute dimensions.

I have a strong appreciation of the merits of MDS. Thus these remarks are meant merely to suggest some probable limits on feasi-

bility in many practical, complex situations and to suggest directions for more efficient utilization of the decision-maker's time.

*Kelly's Role Repertory Test*

The existing methodology that is the most direct parent of that to
be pursued in this book is George Kelly's Role Repertory Test.[11]
It is currently being introduced in England for practical market
research purposes.[12] Kelly's method is potentially extremely flexible. Depending on the situation, it has many of the desirable
properties of either the semantic differential or multidimensional
scaling.

This procedure first asks the decision-maker to match a given
list of object *role* descriptions with appropriate objects from the
decision-maker's own experience. A limited number of triads of
these objects are selected. For each triad, the decision-maker is
first asked which pair of the triad is most similar, and then in *what
important way* the pair is similar with respect to which the third
object is different. This first stage is identical with some forms of
MDS except for the superior way of choosing objects and for the
additional step of eliciting attribute names if available. However,
instead of proceeding to ask for further comparisons among a large
number or among all possible triads of the group of objects, this
first stage is ended at an earlier point and the second stage begun.
Suppose fifteen triad comparisons had been utilized in the first
stage triad comparisons. Kelly gave the objects a score of +1 or −1
familiar objects to either the "similar" or the "different" pole of
each of the fifteen raw attributes implicitly defined by the first

11. See Kelly (1955) and Mair (1967). The Role Repertory Test was originally developed to measure the structure of interpersonal social perceptions.
12. See articles by Lunn (1969) and Morgan and Purnell (1969) detailing uses
and possibilities in market research.

stage triad comparisons. Kelly gave the objects a score of +1 or −1 on each attribute, depending on the pole to which it was assigned. The attribute data thus obtained were then factor analyzed to eliminate redundancies.

The advantages of Kelly's procedure are three. First, the triad similarity comparison task which induces a high work load is made easier by using individualized, self-selected familiar objects. Second, useful information in the form of implicit attribute labels is extracted. Third, the first stage similarity comparison task is cut short after eliciting these labels and a more efficient method utilized to obtain data thereafter.

In the second stage, it is a relatively easy task for the decision-maker to position each object on each relevant attribute scale obtained in the first stage and labeled with his own vocabulary. This permits, in the author's opinion, more accurate and feasible recording of the initial data in most practical cases than does MDS, primarily because we are putting the decision-maker's own subjective and internalized semantic structure to work.[13]

### 3.3. Direct Models of Decision Nets

We have noted that decision nets that optimize may be represented in terms of preference orderings over the available choice set. Those decision nets that do not optimize, however, do not force all alternatives to be considered using only the criteria attributes to define the choice set. Such decision nets may not be precisely representable in terms of a set of alternatives ordered by these attributes. For such decision nets, we would have to know

---

13. This would not be true in those cases where the subject could not be induced to produce signs or labels indicative *to him* of the underlying attribute. However, such cases are rare, if they exist at all.

the information processing procedure embedded in the decision net before we could predict which alternatives would be considered and with what result. In such cases we must first model the decision net directly. Further translating of the direct model of the decision net thus obtained into a set representation would usually be unnecessary to our purposes.

Those who have seriously attempted to model managerial decision-making have discovered that much of it could not be characterized as optimizing. In consequence, the researcher faces two alternatives in modeling such decisions. The first is to proceed with a choice-set representation, knowing well that it offers at best an approximation. The second is to attempt to monitor directly not just the inputs and outputs to the decision but also the information processing activities that mediate them.[14] This has been the method used over the last fifteen years by those following the approach pioneered by H. Simon and his associates.

Thus far, the work in direct modeling of decision nets has been descriptive, rather than normative.

In the line of research carried on by Simon, March, Cyert, and their associates during the late 1950s and early 1960s, a major focus has been on the positive description of decision-making under uncertainty in complex and changing environments. From observing real-life business decisions and the kinds of search activities and information flows which are associated with them, one can draw conclusions as to the goals and structure of each decision and the kind of information system support it requires.[15]

14. See Simon (1955, 1959). Of course, at some level of detail each of these linking or mediating activities might be susceptible to a choice-set representation.
15. See Cyert, Dill, and March (1958), March and Simon (1958), Simon, Cyert, and Trow (1956).

These studies have been influential in changing the generally accepted picture of the manager at work. In the theoretical realm at least, this picture had been dominated by the representation of classical microeconomics. One important result has been the rise of a new set of conceptual tools for analyzing processes of managerial planning and control. These include satisficing, the search for alternatives, heuristics for pruning alternatives, and means-ends decision trees, which are a further development of Von Neumann's structuring of a decision in terms of a hierarchical decision tree or network. This structure was used in Chapter 2. Such concepts have been strongly influenced by concurrent research in developing computer programs that perform intelligently (Newell and Simon 1971). Indeed, a particularly striking study of an investment trust officer by Clarkson (1962) modeled an important decision net so successfully that it could then be very closely duplicated by a computer program.

A second important result has been the development of support research techniques. These emphasize, for the organization, extensive observation of the processes of information gathering and intra-organizational communication. For the individual, intensive use is made of protocols obtained by tape-recording the decision-maker "thinking aloud" while traversing his decision nets as he makes repeated decisions. These techniques, although powerful in the hands of a skilled analyst, remain an art. They also require a very considerable time investment by both the researcher who models and the decision-makers who are modeled.

Given equal theoretical validity, modeling through a preference-ordered choice-set representation is much more practically feasible than direct modeling of the decision net. However, we know that often the choice-set representation is not entirely valid. Thus, a critical question is a method for determining the degree of its validity so that we know in a given case which approach to use. Of course, one can gain some relevant data by attempting a choice-set representation first and then testing the resulting model's predictive power. If it is exceptionally poor, we have a good heuristic indicating the desirability of paying more attention to the actual procedure of information processing in the decision net.

It is thus worthwhile to attempt routinely first a choice-set representation of the decision if the practical feasibility of obtaining such models over that of direct decision net models is sufficiently favorable. In my view, the method for measuring decision assumptions presented in the next chapter improves this feasibility advantage to an extent sufficient to indicate this conclusion. That is, the recommended procedure is to try a choice-set representation first before proceeding, if necessary, to a direct model of the decision net.

## In Summary
We find in the various social sciences a variety of ideas and ideologies regarding the character of decision assumptions. One broad group, typified by economists, is determined to view decision-making through normative eyeglasses. This results in a characteristic distaste for confronting individual decision-makers whose decision processes deviate from the required axioms. I have argued in passing that in a world of necessary cognitive limitations, the normative viewpoint of economics is not always usefully prescriptive for individual decision-makers. Thus this distaste is unwarranted even from those who wish to see no evil. There is much to be gained from an examination of microeconomic axioms, however, in determining when naïve multivariate regression methods are

likely to be successful in determining an adequate choice-set representation of decision assumptions.

Another broad group, typified by applied psychologists, also views decision-making in a choice-set representation, but is unabashedly descriptive in its viewpoint. From their work over the last few decades have come the semantic differential, nonmetric multidimensional scaling, and the role repertory test. These tools are all aimed at solving the problem of misspecification of relevant attributes, which is perhaps the key difficulty in modeling decision assumptions of widely differing individuals.

Finally, some progress has been made by a group of behavioral scientists who reject choice-set representation in favor of a process-oriented decision-net approach. Their work illuminates the reasons underlying errors in measurement often produced through a choice-set representation. On the other hand, it so far offers little hope for practical, routine use.

# II

A Stock Market Participant
Case Study

# 4

## A Method for Measuring Assumptions and Its Application to Stock Market Participants

The method for measuring assumptions which I propose is based on an attempt to combine the most important advantages of the semantic differential, multidimensional scaling, and Kelly's Role Repertory Test. In addition, techniques for better using existing multivariate regression methods in small samples have been included. The method's features are briefly reviewed in Section 4.1. Section 4.2 gives an overview of an extensive study of stock market participants which used this method. Later chapters will use the stock market study to provide examples of the method and its applications.

The reader will find that this chapter begins a transition from discussion of general issues on a rather abstract plane to concrete grappling with specific problems. I regard my own efforts in measuring decision assumptions as experimental in character. The next four chapters describe pragmatic steps which seem to meet the major difficulties found in practice. No doubt, however, as the art is further developed some aspects of the method will be viewed as unnecessary or overly crude.

## 4.1. A Method for Measuring Decision Assumptions

The reader may wish to review Section 3.2 at this point, in order to refresh his memory regarding Kelly's Role Repertory Test. Briefly, the first stage of that procedure elicits from the decision-maker labels for implicit attributes defined by triad groupings.

I have altered Kelly's procedure at the beginning of its second stage by first allowing the decision-maker to divide each of the newly labeled attribute scales into from two to nine equivalence intervals, depending on how fine a discrimination he wishes to make. For each attribute, the objects are then coded with real-number values according to the equivalence interval in which they are assigned. Objects are coded from 0 to 1000. For example, if two equivalence intervals are used, objects are coded either 250 or 750. Separate intervals for "not enough information" or "scale not appropriate" are also provided.[1] These codes are then factor analyzed.

Factor analysis using these data for a single decision-maker thus eliminates most of the previously mentioned difficulties of the semantic differential. This follows since the attributes are much more likely to be relevant, since a separate analysis is run for each decision-maker, and since the factor analysis may be based, if necessary, on purely ordinal data with only two equivalence intervals per scale.[2]

If the decision-maker can distribute, say, twenty objects on a scale divided into five intervals, we obtain a great deal of quasi-metric data from him. Such a task may be nearly equivalent in usefulness to getting him to make all possible (190) pairwise ordinal or even metric comparisons, but it is of much lower cost. When this is not possible, the decision-maker has a tendency to divide the scale less finely. Thus, the methodology does not force metric quantification directly on the decision-maker's initial responses. Further, unlike Kelly's original methods, and unlike multidimensional scaling, it uses as much ordinal or metric information as is available on each attribute scale separately, rather than making one supposition for all attributes.

For each decision-maker, a separate factor analysis is done of the ratings of each object on each implicit attribute elicited and labeled by the decision-maker. This provides the ability to further

1. Special codes are provided for these off-the-scale objects.
2. Purely ordinal data imply factor analysis of dummy variables; this presents some theoretical problems, but in practice factor scores based on such an analysis of real data typically have considerable metric content.

refine the positioning of the objects on new orthogonal attribute factors of higher explanatory power, and also to eliminate redundant attribute labels. The author has successfully used a varimax rotation of principal components as the method of factor analysis, but other reasonable factor analytic procedures could be substituted.[3] In the remainder of this book, the original attributes are termed raw attributes. The summary attribute factors are often referred to merely as attributes.

The obvious next step here would be to use least-squares multiple regression of the objects' factor attribute scores against separate preference ratings for the objects. The regression coefficients would thus represent measures of decision assumptions. If "dummy" decision or preference variables are used, the appropriate procedure may be discriminant analysis.[4]

Herzberg has recently gathered evidence through Monte Carlo simulation that regression of a dependent variable against independent principal components scores usually yields more dependable prediction equations than those estimated directly from a large number of raw variables. The improvement is greatest for regressions using small numbers of observations.[5]

3. See Dixon (1968) and Harman (1967) for further information on factor analysis. Actually, "component analysis" is what is done, since "factor analysis," in the technical sense, would discard any variation present in only a single variable.
4. See Anderson (1958) for an account of discriminant analysis as an alternative to multivariate regression. If the decision result has three or more possibilities which cannot be put on a single scale, or is restricted to a few distinct values, multiway discriminant analysis may be appropriate. Two-way discriminant analysis, however, can be done using a standard regression procedure.
5. See Paul A. Herzberg (1969). See Johnston (1963) for a straightforward discussion of the problem of multicollinearity among the explanatory variables in estimating a least-squares regression model.

I was not aware of Herzberg's results at the time of the stock market study in which the decision assumption measurement methodology was developed. As a result, the following very conservative procedure was constructed. It has certain nonstatistical advantages over his one-step procedure. Rather than rely on a single set of attribute data for both factor analysis and regression coefficient estimation, two separate sets of data are used. From the first set, ratings on each of the raw attributes by the decision-maker are factor analyzed. The factor structure thus obtained is used to transform a second, new set of ratings on the originally elicited raw attribute scales into a set of scores. We shall term these as quasi factor scores. That is, quasi factor scores for the second data set are obtained which are identical to the factor scores that would have been obtained if its sample factor structure were the same as that of the first data set. The mathematics of this transformation is outlined in Appendix A. Derived in this way, the additional regression degrees of freedom created by the data reduction through factor analysis are a priori nonillusory. From a statistical view, since this method does not use all the correlation information in the two samples of data, it is not theoretically optimum. In particular, after following this method the order of the two data sets could then be reversed. The second list of regression coefficients thus obtained could be combined with the first list to produce an improved joint estimate. It may even be that a single-step regression and factor analysis based on a doubly large set of observations, as done by Herzberg, would be more reliable when considered on purely statistical grounds.

However, in the stock market participant study used as context for developing the present method of measuring decision assumptions, the conservative, two-sample approach offered an overriding

advantage. The first set of data could be taken on objects familiar
to the individual decision-maker, but the second set, since the
factor-structure had been already estimated, could be taken using
a common set of objects for a large set of decision-makers. Familiarity with the objects is much more critical in estimating the factor structure than in estimating the consequent regression coefficients relating factor scores to preferences. By using this two-step
procedure, the possibility of detailed comparison of assumptions
among the decision-makers is left open without undue degradation
of the measurement. This is often desirable in practical situations.
However, an improvement, based on my experience in this study,
would be also to collect preference data along with the first data set.

Typical least-squares regression procedures relating the factor
scores or quasi factor scores to the separately measured decision
preference ratings under study would complete the measurement
of decision assumptions. However, when the available degrees of
freedom are few, as they generally are when there are small numbers of observations taken from real managers, problems still occur
in obtaining reliable regression coefficients. Of course, the reliability of the measure can be tested against new data, but my
experience suggests another way. Some reasonable confidence may
be placed in the measure, even if quite small samples of observations are used, if care is taken not to contaminate the analysis. I
used twenty observations for factor analysis and another twenty
for regression estimation for each stock market decision-maker.[6]
The key in such small sample situations is a stringent algorithm for

6. Again, if the stock market study were to be done over, I might well collect
preference data from the beginning. Thus, with minor additional effort, one
could use twenty observations for factor analysis and forty observations for
regression.

obtaining the regression equation with no utilization of subjective judgment. Rather, it utilizes objectively applicable a priori heuristics and statistical tests. In coarse outline, the algorithm suggested is as follows. First, allow factor scores of statistically significant factors only. Second, enter these as variables one at a time into the regression equation in order of descending eigenvalues obtained in the original factor analysis. Third, of course, use a stringent test of statistical significance in the regression before entering the factor into the regression equation. The rare case of serious multicollinearity of the quasi factor scores or the occasional lack of regression significance of any of the estimated factors may be handled by appropriate subalgorithms.

Monte Carlo simulation analysis of the likelihood of eigenvalues obtained through factor analysis of random data is suggested as most feasible for testing factor significance. Also, it may be advantageous to use a regression significance test based on the possibility of errors in the explanatory variables, rather than just in the dependent variable, although my experience did not suggest that this difference is especially critical. On the other hand, the heuristic of using the most important factor first, as measured by its original eigenvalue, does appear to be critical in resolving problems of serious multicollinearity or apparent lack of any factor's contributing to the regression explanation. Also, the use of a predetermined sequence of trials in entering explanatory variables allows a conservative regression significance test which eliminates one degree of freedom for each explanatory variable previously tried, even if it was rejected and is thus not in the present regression equation. This eliminates the fairly well known illusions of inflated significance typically experienced during step-wise regression.[7]

7. These issues are explored in more detail in Chapter 6.

All of these details of my method of measuring decision assumptions are given concrete illustration in the next three chapters.

**A Method for Solving the Interpretability of Dimensions Problem**

In brief, the problem of interpretability of results can be approached through the parallel application of the measurement methodology to both the decision-maker to be measured and the outside observer who wants to interpret the subjective assumptions of the decision-maker. At the point of gathering a second set of data to be transformed into quasi factor scores, both observer and decision-maker use the same real-world referent objects. Thus, two differents sets of quasi factor scores can be derived, based on the same referents. If the interrelationships among these scores are analyzed by the method of canonical correlations, the resulting canonical correlation coefficients provide the best linear mapping of the attributes used by the decision-maker into those used by the observer.[8]

**4.2. Measuring Stock Market Participant Decision Assumptions**

This section relates the general issues discussed in the previous chapters to the specific intent and design of the study of stock market participants to be described in detail in the next three chapters.

Again, an overall aim of this book is to make a contribution toward measurements of managerial assumptions which will make them more tractable for inclusion within explicit managerial planning and control systems. The resulting potential for increased explicitness might then be exploited by managers to improve their own self-observation and learning, and for improved communication. A variety of other academic and practical objectives in the

8. See Anderson (1958) for an exposition of canonical correlation.

social sciences may also be served by success in the measurement of decision assumptions. This section discusses the implied major hypothesis of the study which tested my method of measurement. It also treats the selection of a stock market context for the study and the design of the study's data collection effort.

**Motivation of the Stock Market Participant Study**

One might attempt to make explicit several different parts of the planning and control process: the manager's initial specification of the problem (Pounds 1965), his ultimate objectives, his information processing sequence, or his assumptions. I have chosen to model his decision assumptions through a choice-set representation.[9] These assumptions prescribe the nature of the planning and control process and, even more fundamentally, the events that the manager recognizes as symptomatic of problems to be attacked through this process. Any such data we can gather will be helpful in the application of management science. For example, measures of decision assumptions can help us determine the usefulness of existing accounting information in providing information that management perceives as relevant to management's perceived problems, with consequent education or redesign implications. We can thus conceive of a metacontrol process through which the gap between management information needs and the output provided by the existing information system is minimized. Also, if we can measure these decision assumptions reliably and if we have matching normative criteria, we can sequentially improve fundamental determinants of the planning process underlying the control process and structure of the business organization.

---

9. Note that if we replace preference data by any other attribute data the measurement will be of predictive assumptions rather than decision assumptions.

The problem of developing the appropriate procedures for decision assumption measurement in the field is broader than I have previously implied. It includes —

1. inducing the decision-maker to undertake a known objective,
2. observing and adequately characterizing his means for operating to attain that end,[10]
3. reducing extraneous influences on the measure.

All three of these subproblems present considerable difficulties, especially if the measurement is to be conducted in the rough-and-tumble of the real-world, nonlaboratory environment. However, the major emphasis in my research is on improvements in the second subproblem, observing and adequately characterizing the decision-maker's means to his ends.

**Hypothesis**

The hypothesis of the study was the presumption that it was possible, using the technique already described, to practically measure aspects of a decision-maker's decision assumptions which are important determinants of managerially significant decisions. This hypothesis was to be rejected if the measurement method took too much of the decision-maker's or the observer's time, if it could not be reduced to a concrete recipe, or if it was of no predictive usefulness.

The reasons for choosing ratings of common stocks as a trial case for the method are noted as follows.

**Selection of a Specific Trial Case**

It was desired to make a contribution toward improved measurement procedures which might make data concerning managerial decision assumptions tractable. I judged that in order to have significant real-world impact, such procedures must be much more

10. It is this factor that was mainly discussed in Chapter 3.

reproducible and objective than those extant. The decision net models by Clarkson, for example, appear to require far too much skill and time to construct for widespread managerial use. This judgment suggested the strategic use of a well-specified procedure of statistical estimation.

My objective suggests initial application in a management area that is, though significant, relatively limited in scope. This is because the possible diversity of kinds of assumptions is exceedingly rich. The broader the role across different decision domains of the decision-maker, the more difficult the measurement task becomes. Also, as the number of distinct relevant attributes grows, the number of events from which cognitive assumptions can be deduced for each dimension tends to shrink, making statistical inference more difficult. Furthermore, we must consider the structure of the action space that is governed by the attribute space. This action space reflects the nature of the decision-maker's means. Other things equal, more complicated action sequences require more complicated assumptions and more diverse attributes and are thus more difficult to measure. This need to avoid complication is one reason why the initial emphasis of our decision measures is on the individual decision-maker.

In summary, it is relatively easy to measure reliably the relevant assumptions of a decision-maker who deals with a large number of simple-consequence decisions from the same domain. It is much harder when a decision-maker deals with only a few very large decisions. It is harder when his decisions have very complicated action spaces. It is harder still when his decisions are in different environmental domains. Only after the measurement procedure has been developed under favorable circumstances should extensions into these more difficult areas be attempted.

For these reasons, the empirical part of the research is focused on decision-makers who repeatedly make purchases or purchase recommendations for individual common stocks. This decision ranks favorably on our criteria of measurement difficulty.

Parenthetically, the assumptions to be measured are at two levels in a hierarchical means-end chain:
1. assumptions about the relations between attributes used by the decision-maker to characterize stocks and the decision-maker's outcome preferences according to some investment objective;
2. assumptions as to the position of a particular stock on one of the above attributes.
Our attention in this book is focused mostly on the first level. At the second level, we can say a particular stock is a specific means to an investment objective. But so too, at the more general first level in the means-end hierarchy, we can say that the particular attributes used by the decision-maker to characterize stocks as alternatives, and thus to discriminate among stocks in attempting to gain an investment objective, are general means to the investment objective. It is this more general means-end relationship to which I have referred as a decision assumption.

There are significant advantages in focusing on stock market decision-makers. They make a large number of decisions in a relatively homogeneous domain with a simple action space. In most cases the choice to buy a stock affects the environment that governs later decisions of the same type less significantly than for other kinds of important decisions. This further simplifies the action space and effectively increases the number of independent decisions. Also, cognitive assumptions governing the choice of stocks are presumably relatively peripheral to various social or organization norms that might make a manager unwilling to reveal

himself for measurement. Third, there are large numbers of decision-makers making similar decisions. This makes possible a much
broader class of prescriptive application possibilities than would a
focus on a single decision-maker.

The reader should note that the material used for testing the
measurement methodology pertains to phenomena of interest to
the field of finance. However, it was not intended that this research be a contribution to the normative theory of finance. On
the other hand, it does provide some relevant descriptive data.

I have wished to demonstrate broad applicability of the measurement method, as well as to gather data from large enough
numbers of decision-makers to provide some basis for empirically
based normative judgments. This is partly responsible for the distinct differences in approach between this study and those done
by Clarkson, by Slovic, and by Green and Maleshwari, which also
modeled decision assumptions regarding common stocks.[11] Clarkson, in particular, focused on the modeling of a single individual,
and did not offer a reproducible measurement procedure. Further,
his neglect of statistical estimation methods and lack of extension
to larger numbers of decision-makers made his study difficult to
relate to other studies and existing theory. However, the fortunate
existence of such different, though related, studies provides an
interesting instance for comparison, both in methodology of measurement approach and in findings. This comparison is made in
Chapter 8.

Partly for convenience and partly to avoid distrust by the decision-makers, the study did not attempt to discover what procedures were actually used by organizations and individual partici-

11. See Clarkson (1962), Slovic (1969), and Green and Maheshwari (1969).

pants involved in the stock market, nor to monitor their actual decisions. Instead, a surrogate decision activity, simple rating of stocks according to a specified objective, was used. Such a procedure allows for the study of decisions on more stocks per individual and of many more individuals. It also allows for greater consistency of decision-making conditions among decision-makers, thus reducing "background noise." As an unfortunate side effect, little direct information was gained regarding the kinds of information-search activities which direct decision-net modeling might have revealed. The decision-maker was merely asked to rate stocks using only his available knowledge. Similarly, he was asked to rate stocks along attributes elicited from him using only his available knowledge. Any information-search activities going on were passed over unrecorded.

## Data Collection Design

The research design described in this section was constructed in early 1969. The cooperation of several organizations, such as trust departments, mutual fund advisors, or brokerage houses, was thought to be desirable in order to (1) facilitate contact with individual decision-makers; (2) gain some insight into the homogeneity of conceptual viewpoints within organizations; and (3) increase the potential for useful application of the research findings. However, it should be understood that the subject of the study was not organizational procedures for stock market decision-making. Rather it was the nature, variety, and implications of decision assumptions of individuals as they participate as individuals in the market for particular stocks.

It was thought to be desirable to gather data from at least fifteen subjects within a cooperating organization. Two or three organizations were sought, in order to bring the total sample up to at least forty subjects. Each subject was expected to spend in participation about four hours of his time distributed over a six-month period. Activities which were planned were —

1. a modified stock role repertory exercise;
2. two stock preference rating activities for a limited set of stocks, together with ratings of the stocks along each individual's characteristic attributes derived from the role repertory exercise.

These activities are described briefly in the following paragraphs.

*Stock Role Repertory Exercise*

Again, this is an adaptation of G. A. Kelly's Role Repertory Test (Kelly 1955). A list of twenty "roles" various stocks play in the subject's experience and conceptual structure is prepared. The following are possible examples: "the stock you first made a considerable gain in," "a stock you sold too soon," and "a very popular stock."[1][2] The decision-maker is asked to designate a particular stock for each of these as representative of the role.

Twenty triads, or groups of three, of these stocks are selected. Each triad is then presented to the decision-maker. He is asked in what important way two of these stocks are similar with respect to which the third is different. This procedure elicits labels of important conceptual dimensions or attributes along which the subjects perceive stocks.

The stock role repertory exercise may be done in an interview requiring from sixty to ninety minutes. The remainder of the data collection is done through a series of written questionnaires at later times.

The first questionnaire gives the elicited raw attributes and asks the decision-maker to do the following for each such attribute.

12. See Chapter 5 for details.

First, divide the scale into between two and nine equivalence intervals. Second, place any appropriate stocks into two separately provided categories, "scale not relevant," and "not enough information." Third, place the remaining stocks on the attribute scale in their appropriate intervals.

*Stock Rating Activities*

The second questionnaire presents blank scales for each of the elicited attributes. These scales are divided into the intervals into which the decision-maker had previously segmented them. Then he is asked to place each of a new, standardized list of relatively well-known stocks on each dimension or in the "scale not relevant" or "not enough information" categories. All decision-makers are given the same list of stocks for this activity.

In the third questionnaire, the decision-maker rates the same new, standardized list in terms of some particular investment objective, which he is allowed to select. He is free to use any relevant information which he might possess.

After an interval of about three months, the fourth and fifth questionnaires repeat the second and third questionnaires, respectively, for a similar standardized list of stocks. These fourth and fifth questionnaires are not part of the initial assumption measure but rather a test of its validity.

This data collection design allows a test of the hypothesis that the measurement procedures utilized have value in predicting decision-makers' subsequent ratings. That is, the test proceeds in two stages. In the first, one estimates relationships between each decision-maker's ratings of stocks along various characterizing attributes and his ratings of the same stock along his own selected investment objective. This estimating procedure utilizes the results of the stock role repertory exercise. In the second, one validates these estimated relationships in a repetition with new data (Questionnaires 4 and 5). Of course, this hypothesis test is conservative; the test can fail not only because the measure and implied theory might be inadequate, but also because the decision-maker might change his assumptions during the period between the estimating and validating questionnaires. On the other hand, if the test shows the measure to have been a success, we can reasonably infer that improvements in the decision-maker's consistency or in shortening the time interval would make the results even better.

The assertion was earlier made that it would be possible to specify the modeling procedure to such an extent that it would be readily reproducible. This implies that the researcher's particularized subjective knowledge of each subject, gained in interviewing, for example, *not* be utilized in the model-making process. In the next chapter, the procedures used are specified in such detail as to be, in this view, readily reproducible.

At the time of research design for the study, it was felt that any or all of the following methods of analysis might be appropriate to some extent in estimating the assumption-predicting models for each subject from Questionnaires 2 and 3, using the choice-set representation (Alker 1969):

1. multivariate least-square regression;
2. analysis of variance and covariance;
3. interaction-seeking regression (AID);
4. cluster analysis.

The extent to which all subjects or various classes of subjects are susceptible to predictive modeling based on, say, simple least-squares regression, might in itself be a valuable indication of the kinds of processes which link cognitive maps to resulting decision actions. A priori, the hierarchical decision trees suggested by

Clarkson's study would indicate the potential usefulness of inter-action-seeking regression, or analysis of covariance, as opposed to simple regression in linking preference data with the attribute data. In addition, it might well be that various measures of attribute scale orthogonality, scale polarity, etc., derivable from analyzing Questionnaire 1, would be useful in postulating initial models for estimation for each decision-maker. Finally, work by Lavin (1969) has suggested that introspective weighting of attributes by the decision-maker could provide a basis for useful prediction of the effect of his assumptions on his preferences.

However, in the course of the study it became apparent that such a full exploration of the relative merits of different modeling procedures would put the study beyond the first-round capabilities of a single researcher with limited resources. It appeared that it was thus wise to narrow the total problem to the attack on better choice-set representation and its basic use.

Accordingly, in the research reported here, the entire emphasis was put on a single well-specified modeling procedure, described in the preceding section. This method focuses on linear multivariate regression of the preference data against the attribute data, using a choice-set representation. Experimentation with more advanced means of exploiting these data is yet to be done.

### In Summary

The most popular existing methods of eliciting relevant attributes and measuring decision assumptions had seemed capable of improvement. Both the semantic differential and multidimensional scaling appeared to require too much work by the individual decision-maker in moderately complicated situations where the observer was unfamiliar with the relevant attributes. With some minor modifications, Kelly's role repertory test seemed to overcome these difficulties. In linking attributes with preferences of real-life managers, however, it is difficult to obtain large numbers of observations. Thus, techniques to increase the available degrees of freedom in multivariate regression must be resorted to. These may include factor analysis to condense the independent variables, rejection of insignificant factors as explanatory variables, and reliance on the factors with largest eigenvalues.

In order to test these methods in favorable circumstances, it was deemed desirable to focus on rather repetitive decisions carried out by a large number of decision-makers. Thus, a study was designed using participants in the stock market. The detailed description of the outcome of this study in the next three chapters provides an explicit handbook for the reader's guidance in his own field of application.

# 5

Measuring Market Participant
Assumptions — Eliciting
Attribute Scales

In Chapters 5, 6, and 7, a detailed narrative is given of the results of the empirical research procedure used in this study of stock market participants. This material is in three main parts: (1) eliciting attribute scales, (2) algorithmic estimation of decision assumptions, and (3) predictive validation of assumption measures. These chapters are intended to convey an operational description of the measurement procedure sufficiently concrete to serve as a handbook or a manual for the reader's own applications.

Chapter 5 describes the interviews in which the role repertory test is administered, the postinterview processing of the tape-recorded interview to obtain raw attribute labels, Questionnaire 1, and the factor analysis of Questionnaire 1 data to determine factor attributes. The section on factor analysis is mildly technical and can be omitted up to Table 5.7 at first reading.

## 5.1. The Interviews

In November 1968, the first of forty subjects was secured and interviewed. The interviewing process, thus begun, continued through May 1969; the bulk of the interviewing was done in March and April. The long delay from first to last interview was by no means a result of the difficulty of the interview or of the interview analysis procedure. An average of about one subject per day could be interviewed and the subsequent tape recording processed. Rather, the difficulty lay mainly in getting cooperating organizations. Only one financial institution could reasonably be said to have fulfilled the planned large quota of decision-makers per organization. However, a number of financial institutions contributed a few each. In addition, twelve individual private investors were added to the sample to bring it up to forty participants.

These were categorized as follows:

12  individual investors

9  large fund portfolio managers and senior investment officers

5  individual trust officers

7  security analysts and junior investment officers

6  quantitative investment analysts

1  professional trader.

These decision-makers are not identified further in order to preserve their anonymity. Hereafter, each decision-maker is referred to by his number, for example, Subject No. 22 or Subject 22.

It should be noted that since a subject's participation was voluntary, the sample was in no sense a random sample of participants in the stock market. However, it was intended that the decision-makers should represent a wide range in organizational roles, market decision activity, and states of well-informedness.

The interviews averaged about 75 minutes in length, with a low of 45 minutes and an upper bound of about 120 minutes. Each participant was interviewed alone. After a brief introduction and description of the research purpose, he was engaged in a stock role repertory exercise (as described in the previous chapter). The equipment required for the exercise consisted of pen, twenty plain cards numbered from one to twenty, and a cassette tape recorder.

The subject was first shown the list of roles in Table 5.1. He was asked to write down the names of appropriate stocks on the corresponding numbered cards, with the restriction that no stock could be used on more than one card.

A few of the individual investors had difficulty in thinking of twenty different stocks which seemed to fit the roles well. However, none of the professional market participants had this difficulty, although some of them expressed frustration at not being

Table 5.1
Stock Role List
_____
1. The stock in which you first made a substantial profit
2. The stock in which you first took a substantial loss
3. Your present favorite stock
4. The stock you most dislike
5. A stock which has gone up significantly
6. A stock which has fallen significantly
7. A very popular stock
8. A stock which may become a good buy sometime in next year
9. A stock a friend likes which you don't like
10. A stock you like which a friend doesn't like
11. A stock you know little about
12. A stock recommended to you by a knowledgeable person
13. A stock which you would recommend to others
14. A stock which might make a good short sale
15. A stock whose market action you feel you understand
16. A stock whose market action is hard to understand
17. A stock which you should have sold sooner
18. A stock which you should have bought sooner
19. A stock which you should have waited longer to sell
20. A stock which you should have waited longer to buy
_____

able to use the same stock in several different places. A sample size
of twenty stocks was chosen, somewhat arbitrarily, because it
seemed like a reasonable compromise between two goals. First, it
was desired not to have so many stocks that the interview would
be too long. Second, it was necessary to avoid having so few that
the factor analysis described later in this chapter would not be
based on sufficient observations to be of some value in summarizing the raw attribute data.

Typical lists of stocks elicited in this manner are shown in Table
5.2. For example, Subject 38 wrote Loew's Theatres on the card

Table 5.2.
Typical Lists of Stocks Elicited

Subject No. 19, May 15, 1969, an individual investor:

1. Long Island Lighting
2. Tri-Continental Warrants
3. Shell Transport and Trading
4. Brooklyn Union Gas
5. American Greetings Corp.
6. Nortek
7. I.B.M.
8. Bow Valley
9. Pet Inc.
10. Avco
11. Avnet
12. Lehman Corp.
13. Federated Department Stores
14. Food Fair
15. Public Service of Colorado
16. Brunswick
17. Anglo-Lautro
18. Tri-Continental Common
19. Dexter Corp.
20. Hawaiian Airlines

Subject No. 38, May 27, 1969, a mutual fund portfolio manager:

1. Rexall
2. Asamera
3. Benguet
4. Marcor
5. Del Webb
6. Leasco
7. Atlantic Ref.
8. National General
9. Loew's Theatres
10. Pacific Petrol
11. Std. Oil of N.J.
12. Memorex
13. Mobil Oil
14. Parvin Dorhman
15. Newmont Mining
16. Natomas
17. U.S. Industries
18. Std. Oil of Indiana
19. General Motors
20. Amrep

marked "a stock a friend likes which you don't like." At this point in the interview, the sound tape recorder was turned on. The subject was presented with three cards at a time, each labeled with a stock. He was asked to group the two that were most similar, and to discuss his reasons for the grouping. This was repeated for twenty sets of three cards. He was allowed to mention anything he felt was important about the stocks, but was encouraged to utilize the procedure of sorting the triad to structure his discussion.

Table 5.3.
List of Triads to be Sorted

| | | | |
|---|---|---|---|
| 1—4—15 | 6—19—10 | 11—8—15 | 16—4—11 |
| 2—6—19 | 7—9—10 | 12—2—1 | 17—20—18 |
| 3—4—14 | 8—3—5 | 13—18—17 | 18—2—9 |
| 4—2—11 | 9—10—5 | 14—12—13 | 19—3—11 |
| 5—7—8 | 10—17—4 | 15—6—16 | 20—12—3 |

The triads in Table 5.3 were utilized. They were selected so as to provide an even distribution and to allow the possibility of stimulating comparisons between certain of the roles on the role list. For example, the first triad groups "the stock in which you first made a substantial profit" with "the stock you most dislike" and with "a stock whose market action you feel you understand."

The excerpts in Table 5.4, transcribed from tape recordings of the session, are typical responses to this exercise. It should be noted that the total quantity of verbal data gathered was about twenty times this great for each decision-maker. Forty subjects were interviewed.

## 5.2. Postinterview Data Processing

The rather voluminous data of the foregoing kind were processed by listening to the tape recordings of the interviews. The processing consisted of taking notes of the type shown in Table 5.5, which correspond to the transcription excerpts given earlier. After processing each of twenty sorts for the subject in this way, a consolidated list of apparent attribute dimensions used by the subject was drawn up. Attributes with only one pole labeled were completed with "not so" on the other pole. Such examples may be found in Appendix C. Some judgment was required here in eliminating nearly equivalent attribute labels. A large number of

Table 5.4.
Sample Interview Transcript Excerpts

Subject No. 37, May 20, 1969, a security analyst, sorting Falstaff Brewing, Needham Packing, and Digital Equipment:

*Subject:* In a vague way you can organize these according to their business, again, Falstaff Brewing and Needham Packing both being in segments of the food industry, Digital Equipment involved in computer applications. The — I would look next at management, and because Digital is one I'm not close to, I can't evaluate their management. Falstaff, again, is weak, here, and Needham is new and untested, operating — it's a company that has a concept and is trying to develop it. I don't think these fall together very neatly in any respect. . . .

*Researcher:* How would that affect your attitude toward a stock to know it was, let's say, computer versus food?

*Subject:* Again, to answer that I would try to quantify the growth rate, the growth potential, of their industries, and I know that the computer — that the segment of the computer business that Digital is in — has a very rapid growing potential, as opposed to the brewing industry, which is perhaps 12 percent to 15 percent a year, and the meat packing business, which *could be* in the 15 percent range also, which Needham's concepts proved realistic. So the answer is — you would think that if, all things being equal, that Digital would have a greater potential, but on the other side if they don't — if they're not a quality management and so on, there could be much greater risk as well.

Subject No. 38, May 27, 1969, a mutual fund portfolio manager, sorting Asamera Oil, Leasco, and General Motors:

*Subject:* General Motors is a stock we sold too soon; we bought that stock in the market decline in 1962 — the stock of Asamera is comparable to that because Asamera is a stock that a long time ago I bought and lost money in. I bought it at 3/16 and sold it at 2/16. Of course, today it is trading in the high 30s and it is one of the big participants in the supposed big oil find in Indonesia.

*Researcher:* Do you see any comparison between Asamera and General Motors now, or are they different?

*Subject:* No, I think they're very different now. General Motors I think of as representative of a certain kind of investment stock, the growth stock of the thirties and forties, if you will. Asamera is a stock which has come from the ranks of being a rank speculation to being a rank speculation that has appreciated a great deal.

In a somewhat facetious way, the managements of the two companies are perhaps comparable, because you can't trust either of them.*

*Researcher:* How does Leasco fit into the picture?

*Subject:* Well, Leasco is regarded by the establishment as being a very low grade, low quality stock of the Asamera variety, where basically through "manipulation," "untested management" has acquired a medium-sized, second-line insurance company, simply by printing paper. Now this is maybe the same thing Asamera is trying to do, because now that their stock has run up on these Indonesian oil discoveries, they're going to try to sell stock, — a rights offering —.

*Researcher:* Do you view Leasco in the same way the establishment does?

*Subject:* No. To date, the company's [Leasco's] earnings projections have been accurate, the company has maintained the earning growth rate projected by its management, which to date is running close to 50 percent per annum. The success of the company is largely dependent on its continuing ability to make acquisitions — and this ability is largely dependent on the price of its stock — so Leasco is very much a child of the market.

---

* This is the subject's opinion, not necessarily the author's.

attributes is desirable in order not to miss any distinctions the subject might be making. However, too many near-duplicates make the succeeding questionnaire rating tasks too tedious for the subject. The general rule followed was not to eliminate possible duplicates whenever one might reasonably conjecture a distinction. There was typically about a thirty percent reduction in number of attribute labels at this stage. The resulting lists of raw, or implicit, attribute labels were incorporated into Questionnaire 1.

These role repertory exercises appeared to elicit notably individualized attribute categorizations. As the reader will note from Table 5.4, the decision-maker was allowed to digress from this format to bring out his interests. However, the triad confrontations which forced categorization were often the underlying stimulus for even these "digressions." In my judgment, the interviewer's resisting the temptation to impose his own categorizations on the decision-maker's response is an important determinant of overall success.

## 5.3 Questionnaire 1, Procedure and Results

The decision-maker, in filling out Questionnaire 1, used the same list of stocks that he had written down on cards in the preceding

Table 5.5.
Sample Postinterview Processing Notes

Subject No. 37:

Falstaff

Needham                                              Digital Equipment

  food                                               computer
  industry                                           applications

Falstaff

  weak
  management

Needham

  New, untested management
  has a concept, trying
  to develop it

Falstaff
Needham                                              Digital Equipment

  slower                                             market growth
                                                     very rapid

                                                     high growth potential

Subject No. 38:

*Sort 2*

General Motors                                       Leasco
Asamera Oil

Asamera Oil                                          General Motors

  a rank                                             growth stock of
  speculation                                        the 30s and 40s
                                                     (one class of investment)

Asamera
General Motors

  you can't
  trust
  management

Asamera
Leasco

  run-up stock used
  for new acquisitions

| | |
|---|---|
| Leasco _____ | |
| Asamera | |
|    regarded by<br>   establishment _____<br>   as low quality | |
| Leasco_____ | |
|    stock down     _____<br>   very substantially | |
|    earnings projections _____<br>   have been accurate | |
|    company has maintained a _____<br>   high growth rate | |
|    company whose success is _____<br>   dependent on acquisitions | |

interview. The questionnaire was typically mailed to each subject about one week after his interview. The subject was given the directions shown in Appendix B.

Between twenty and forty-five pairs of raw attribute labels, one label for each end of the scale, were used in preparation of the subject's questionnaire. The exact number of pairs used depended on the earlier processing of the recorded interview.

Armed with directions and the list of stocks, the subject applied himself to a multipage questionnaire that had five raw attribute label pairs per page of the following type.

1. Good                                      Poor
   management                                management

                     Scale does      |      Not enough
                     not apply        |      information

An example of one page of responses by one subject is shown in Table 5.6. The numbers stand for the stocks the decision-maker offered in response to the role repertory exercise.

Table 5.6
A Sample Response to Questionnaire 1

S. no. 37

| 1. | 15, 5, 7, 11, 12, 18 | 3, 6, 16, 17 | 10, 14, 8, 19 | 2, 4 |
|----|----------------------|--------------|---------------|------|
| | well managed | | | poorly managed |
| | | | | 9, 1, 20 |
| | | | Scale does not apply | Not enough information |

| 2. | 5, 7, 3, 15, 11 | 14, 17, 19, 18 | 10, 13, 8, 16 | 4, 2 |
|----|-----------------|----------------|----------------|------|
| | a leader in its business | | | a weak competitor in its industry |
| | | | 12, 1, 6 | 9, 20 |
| | | | Scale does not apply | Not enough information |

| 3. | 15, 5, 7, 17 | 11, 1, 19, 16, 13, 10, 12 | 6, 8, 18, 14, 4, 2 | |
|----|--------------|---------------------------|--------------------|---|
| | deep management | | | thin management |
| | | | | 9, 20 |
| | | | Scale does not apply | Not enough information |

| 4. | 5, 7, 15, 18, 14, 13, 12, 17, 6 | 2, 3, 8, 10, 16, 19 | 4 |
|----|---------------------------------|---------------------|---|
| | well-structured organization | | poorly structured organization |
| | | | 11, 20, 9, 1, 7 |
| | | Scale does not apply | Not enough information |

| 5. | Same as 3 |
|----|-----------|
| | well grounded in management techniques ... not well grounded in management techniques |

| | Scale does<br>not apply | Not enough<br>information |
|---|---|---|

Key for Stocks
1.  Avco
2.  Needham Packing
3.  Winnebago Industries
4.  Falstaff Brewing
5.  IBM
6.  Monogram
7.  Xerox
8.  Green Giant
9.  Maine Sugar Industries
10. Iowa Beef
11. Digital Equipment Corp.
12. Fuqua
13. Wilson
14. Coleman
15. Anheuser
16. Heublein
17. General Mills
18. Pabst
19. United Fruit
20. Sundstrand

Thus, for example, Subject No. 37 felt that Needham Packing, the stock in which he first took a substantial loss, was a "weak competitor in its industry."

These data from Questionnaire 1 were coded on punched cards. The codes ran on a scale from 0 to 1000 for each attribute. In the example shown by Table 5.6 for the raw attribute "a leader in its business versus a weak competitor in its industry," stock number 18 was coded 375, stock number 2 was coded 875, and so on. The three stocks placed in "Scale does not apply" were coded 499. The two stocks placed in "Not enough information" were coded 501. Any omitted stocks, or stocks used more than once, would have been coded 502. Thus, the special codes 499, 501, and 502, being close to the center of the scale, could be included in later processing with a typically small error, or they could be used to select cases for special processing or to be omitted from regular processing.

Why was a three-digit code used? It is desirable to preserve in the coded data some information from the questionnaire regarding the physical distance between the centers of each content-equivalence interval which the subject had specified for each scale. For example, if the subject divides a raw attribute scale into only two content-equivalence intervals, stocks placed in one of them are coded either 250 or 750, with a maximum distance between different codes. If the subject divided the scale into three intervals, stocks were coded on that scale by 167, 500, or 833, somewhat closer together. If, for example, one wanted to compare the polarization of stocks on different scales, this information might well be useful. In addition, a three-digit code allowed special codes close to 500, the middle of the scale, for the reasons just cited. The addition to the code of the last two digits allowed both preserving the inter-interval "distance" information and combining special codes with the regular data unobtrusively.

An important point to note is that all stocks placed within a given interval, as are stocks 15, 5, 7, and 17 in attribute 3, "deep management versus thin management," in the foregoing example, were coded with the same number — in that case, 125. No information about the place of the stock within the interval has been preserved; this is what is meant by "content-equivalence interval."

The subject's categorization of a stock into content-equivalence intervals has been coded as a cardinal integer. Of course, data along a single attribute scale have more or less metric implications, depending on the number of intervals into which the subject has divided the attribute line. Even leaving aside the complications raised by the special code categories, a scale having only two main equivalence intervals can only express an ordinal comparison, whether or not one chooses to code the responses cardinally. Three intervals, on the other hand, carry some *ordinal metric* information, and higher numbers of distinct intervals on a scale can carry more and more nearly *cardinal metric* information.[1]

No claim is made that codes used carry a perfect cardinal metric. Rather, in this view, they often carry *some* cardinally metric information. The process of determining factor measures, to be described in the following section, allows the aggregate construction of a scale out of a number of raw attribute scales combined. In this view, these constructed scales carry a substantial degree of cardinality.

The real proof of this assertion lies in the test of Chapter 7. There it will be shown that measured assumptions can be predicted using standard statistical procedures based on these aggregations of partly ordinal data.

Again, let us repeat this idea. In the modeling process to be described in the remainder of this chapter and in Chapters 6 and 7, it will be demonstrated that it is possible to utilize these data fruitfully in statistical modeling procedures which are more typically used for real number data. One of the chief devices utilized is the construction of "factor measures" (Harman, 1967) which are estimated as linear combinations of the codes on the raw attribute scales. That is, we have

$$F_{ki} = \alpha_{k1} X_{1i} + \ldots + \alpha_{kj} X_{ji} + \ldots + \alpha_{kn} X_{ni}.$$

Here $F_{ki}$ is the factor measure of factor attribute $k$ for the $i$th stock; $X_{ji}$ is the coded value for the $i$th stock on the $j$th raw data attribute. Finally, $\alpha_{kj}$ is the appropriate real number aggregation weight, whose estimation is explained in Chapter 6. In general, if there are $l_j$ equivalence intervals for raw data attribute $X_j$, there are between $\max_j l_j$ and $\Sigma_{j=1}^{n} l_j$ equivalence intervals for each

1. See Georgescu-Roegen (1954).

$F_k$. This increase in the number of equivalence intervals gives the factor measure greater potential for cardinal measurability than has any individual raw data attribute.

No claim is made at this point that the particular factor measures $F_k$ to be estimated have any necessary relevance for our problem of decision assumption measurement. That will come later. It is merely being noted here that such $F_k$ have desirable properties as measures.

Questionnaire 1 was processed by leaving in, and thus muddying the waters, all the special code cases. From Questionnaire 1 was calculated a correlation matrix of the resulting raw data codes for each subject. This correlation matrix $|r_{jj}'|$, where $r_{jj}'$ represents the correlation of the codes along attribute $X_j$ with the codes along attribute $X_j'$, was used in two ways. First, it was used in further eliminating, for succeeding questionnaires, near-duplicate raw attributes. Second, it was factor analyzed.

Subject responses in Questionnaire 1 indicated that some decision-makers found the stock rating process somewhat arduous. A few of them reported spending over two hours in its completion. It was, therefore, deemed important to shorten the questionnaire further. Eliminating raw attributes that seemed to depend on others more concrete, or that were apparently mere synonyms as shown by highly correlated attribute clusters, reduced the number of attributes about fifteen percent further. Parenthetically, the consequent missing data in later questionnaires for whole raw attribute scales were coded by zeros in determining factor measure scores (attribute factor scores). This changed the mean and variance of the factor measures from what would have otherwise been their form, but did not affect the analysis carried out based on them.

## 5.4 Factor Analysis of Questionnaire 1 Data

The coded questionnaires were subject to factor analysis (the reader who is not familiar with this technique should consult Harman 1967). Since each decision-maker had used his own repertory list of twenty stocks, a separate factor analysis for each subject was not only desirable but necessary. The factor analysis was conducted with principal components analysis followed by an orthogonal rotation according to the varimax criterion; the BioMed (BMD) statistical analysis package (Dixon 1968) was used.

This method of factor analysis was taken for the reasons discussed by Harman. It is relatively easy to compute on a large-scale computer. The principal components analysis produces a maximally parsimonious description of the data. The varimax criterion rotation retains much of this parsimony, but sacrifices some of it to produce factors that are easier to interpret. This ease results because loadings for each raw attribute are concentrated on a few factors and vice versa. In addition, in my experience, varimax estimates from structured real-world data are somewhat more robust in the presence of small-sample error than are principal component estimates. No other factor analysis method appeared to have any strong and relevant comparative advantage.

For the reader's convenience, some of the terminology and rationale of factor analysis is reviewed in the following paragraphs. Let $X_{ji}$ be the $i$th observation along the $j$th raw attribute. In the factor analysis, weights $a_{jk}$, often called *factor loadings*, are estimated for each of $n$ normalized raw attribute variables,

$$z_{ji} = \frac{X_{ji} - \overline{X}_j}{\hat{\sigma}\,(X_j)},$$

where

$$\overline{X}_j = \frac{1}{n} \sum_i X_{ji}, \qquad \hat{\sigma}\,(X_j) = \frac{1}{n-1} \sqrt{\sum_i (X_{ji} - \overline{X}_j)^2}\,.$$

Here, $j = 1, \ldots, n$ is the index of the raw attribute variable, and $i = 1, \ldots, N$ is the index of the observation. Using the $a_{jk}$, the $z_{ji}$ can be expressed as linear functions of common underlying factor attributes $F_k$. For principal component analysis, we would have as a result for the $i$th observation,[2]

$$z_{ji} = a_{j1} F_{1i} + a_{j2} F_{2i} + \ldots + a_{jk} F_{ki} + \ldots + a_{jM} F_{Mi}.$$

Typically in our small sample study for each decision-maker, principal component analysis produces $M = N$ estimated factor loadings and factor scores for each normalized raw data attribute.[3] For rotated factors derived from the principal components, we would have new factors and factor loadings:

$$z_{ji} = b_{j1} G_{1i} + b_{j2} G_{2i} + \ldots + b_{jk} G_{ki} + \ldots + b_{jm} G_{mi} + U_{ji},$$

where $m$, $m < M$, is the number of factors estimated and $U_{ji}$ is an error term. Note that the $b_{jk}$ and $G_{ki}$ terms are not the same as those estimated in the immediately preceding equation. In most applications of factor analysis, both the $a_{jk}$ and the $F_{ki}$ (or the $b_{jk}$ and $G_{ki}$) are estimated from the sample data $X_{ji}$. Since there is an infinite number of sets of factor loadings and factor scores which satisfy such a set of equations, we must have a criterion for choice

---

2. Note that the $a_{jk}$ are not the same as the $\alpha_{kj}$ of Section 5.3.
3. The index $M$ is the number of factors required to explain the data. Of course, $M$ cannot extend the number of observations $N$ from which the estimate is made if the $F_k$ vectors are to be orthogonal. Typically, in principal components analysis, $M$ is the lesser of $N$ or the number of raw variables, $n$.

among them. The principal components solution criterion is the property that all $M$ vector factor measures $\overline{F}_k = \{F_{ki}\}$, $i = 1, \ldots,$ $N$, are orthogonal[4] to one another, and the further property that $\overline{F}_1$ explains a maximum of the total variance across all the normalized raw data attributes, $\overline{F}_2$ a maximum of the remainder, and so on.

These restrictions define a unique solution for the factor loadings, $\{a_{jk}\} = \mathbf{A}$, such that $\mathbf{Z} = \mathbf{AF}$, in matrix notation.

The solution matrix $\mathbf{A}$ may be used as a starting point to be rotated in factor space until it best satisfies the varimax criterion, which, starting from the full set of principal components, reduces to maximizing the following expression (Harman 1967):

$$V = n \sum_{k=1}^{M} \sum_{j=1}^{n} (b_{jk})^4 - \sum_{k=1}^{M} \left( \sum_{j=1}^{n} b_{jk}^2 \right)^2$$

where $b_{jk}$ is one of the new, rotated factor loadings. That is, a matrix $\mathbf{B} = \mathbf{AT}$, $\mathbf{T}$ an orthogonal transformation matrix, is found such that the $b_{jk}$ satisfy the above criterion. This rotated solution has the desirable property that factor loadings are much more likely than in the principal components solution to be either very large or near zero. Again, this provides a kind of "simple structure" in which the variability of each raw data attribute may be mostly explained in terms of a few factors, and vice versa.

The factor measures derived from these rotated factors are, in most of the remainder of this work, termed individually, $F_k$. However, in Appendix A, they are termed collectively in matrix form $\mathbf{G}$ to distinguish them from the principal components $\mathbf{F}$. If all the

---

4. This means no one $\overline{F}_k$ can be expressed as a linear aggregation of the others.

principal components are rotated, we have in matrix notation not only $\mathbf{Z} = \mathbf{AF}$, but also $\mathbf{Z} = \mathbf{BG}$.[5]

Because the number of observations for each subject was small, $N = 20$, the standard error obtained for individual factor loadings was large, estimated at about 0.3 (Harman 1967). The large size of this expected error reflects the fact that the loadings are small sample estimates.

Thirty-nine subjects completed Questionnaire 1; a summary of the structure of the significant resulting rotated factor estimates for selected subjects is given in Appendix C. This is one of the principal data collection results of the present research.

Only principal components explaining more than $1/n$ of the total normalized variance (eigenvalues greater than unity) were rotated, with a cutoff maximum of ten factors being rotated.[6] For each estimated factor, only the raw attributes having loadings greater than 0.7 (well over twice the probable standard deviation) are shown in Appendix C. The fraction of the total normalized variance explained by a factor can be obtained by dividing the eigenvalue $E_k$ of the factor by the value of $n$. Examples are given in Table 5.7 and in Appendix C.

The factor loadings shown at the left in Table 5.7 and the Appendix C tables represent the correlation of each raw attribute with the summarizing factor attribute. That is, the factor loadings give the correlation coefficient ($r_{jk} = a_{jk}$) between the normalized raw data attribute $z_j$ and the attribute factor measure $F_k$. Labels for both poles of each relevant raw attribute are given, because one pole is not always objectively inferrable from its opposite. The

5. The estimation of $\{\alpha_{kj}\}$ as used in Section 5.3 is explained in Appendix A, using this terminology.
6. The value of $n$ is the number of raw attribute variables for each decision-maker.

starred (*) attribute scales included in the tables were those eliminated in later questionnaires. Again, it should be noted that the
loadings are merely sample estimates of the population loadings.
The method used for determining factor significance which determined which factors were included for each decision-maker in
Appendix C is described in the next section. In order to avoid
undue subjectivity by the investigator, the factors were left un-
named. Factors that did not pass the significance criterion set up
in the following chapter are marked not significant. The example
shown in Table 5.7 is typical; it refers to a single decision-maker.
The pole at the left represents a greater positive value for the
factor measure. That is, a stock characterized by the *left-hand*
labels would be given a high positive score for the factor measure.

Two notes are in order concerning the results of the factor
analysis. First, only the statistically significant factors are relatively dependable as nonrandom indicators of some conceptual
dimension summarizing more than one raw data attribute. The
other factors might either be confirmed, drastically modified, or
denied if the observation sample were enlarged.

Second, even a brief glance through Appendix C will demonstrate very great differences among decision-makers in this mapping of conceptual dimensions. The example for Subject 19 shown
in Table 5.7, though in some sense typical, should not be general-
ized without reference to the other factor structures in the Appendix.

In the next chapters it is demonstrated that the approach taken
for ascertaining the relevant attributes has some merit. There is no
doubt that in specific cases it may be improved upon, sometimes
dramatically. However, I would contend that it is a most appropriate basis, or starting point, for a general method of measurement to be applied routinely to a large variety of problems.

Table 5.7
Factor Structure for Subject 19
_____
Subject 19, an individual investor, $n$ = 35:

Factor I, $E$ = 6.6

| | |
|---|---|
| .74 serves a declining market | serves rapidly growing market |
| .73 not so | sophisticated in the use of financial instruments |
| .87 growth record is poor | growth record is good |
| * .82 has saturated its market | not so |
| * .81 not solid | solid |
| .84 mgmt. not very capable | has very capable mgmt. |
| .88 moves into innovations far behind competition | moves into innovations far ahead of competitors |

Factor II, $E$ = 3.2

| | |
|---|---|
| .92 stock's previous lower level was from nonrecurrent event | stock's previous higher level was from nonrecurrent event |

Factor III, $E$ = 4.6

| | |
|---|---|
| .93 not a regulated utility | a regulated utility |
| .73 diversified product line | single product line |
| * .85 not so | hard hit by high interest rates |

Factor IV, $E$ = 4.1

| | |
|---|---|
| .78 stock has recently been performing worse than others in its group | stock has recently been performing better than others in its group |
| .93 stock has fallen rapidly in last six months | stock has risen rapidly in last six months |
| * .87 in process of being re-evaluated downward | in process of being re-evaluated upward |

Factor V, $E$ = 2.4, not significant (N. Sig.)†

| | |
|---|---|
| .83 listed on major exchange | over the counter |
| .77 not so | price has remained at the same level for last 2 or 3 years |

**Factor VI, $E$ = 3.1**

| .95 few factors affecting profit are outside company's control | many factors affecting company profit are outside company's control |
| .70 would be hard hit by inflation | a hedge against inflation |

**Factor VII, $E$ = 3.8**

| .73 basic commodity product (demand not volatile) | product demand is volatile |
| .72 I know and have investigated myself | not so |
| .85 not so | involved in foreign operations |
| .78 stock price governed by real, underlying forces | stock price governed by paper forces, incestuous rumors |

**Factor VIII, $E$ = 1.9, N. Sig.**

| .84 stock very low compared to where it has been until recently | stock very high compared to where it has been until recently |

**Factor IX, $E$ = 1.4, N. Sig.**

| .89 expresses concern for stockholders | not so |

† This factor is not statistically significant as measured by the significance test constructed in the next section. This does not imply the factor has no interest.

Parenthetically, the patterns of factor loadings shown in Appendix C could have been used to generate factor score estimates $F_{ki}$ for each stock in the subject's original repertory; these latter data, however, were not used in the study described here and have not yet been analyzed. Only the factor loading estimates were used further.

That is, as is discussed in the following chapter, it was the factor structure (pattern of loadings) itself that was put to use for estimating the assumption measured. An alternative approach in a better-known situation would be to collect preference data on the

original repertory stocks. Then the assumptions could be estimated directly.[7]

**In Summary**
Straightforward questioning of decision-makers as to what attributes they use in coming to a decision is often unworkable because they themselves don't know. However, by getting the decision-maker to compare the intersimilarities of familiar alternatives
a few at a time, specific pertinent semantic structures are exercised
and can be identified and labeled. This is done through the role
repertory test.

   Those structures of raw attributes which are not adequately dif-
ferentiated to provide a cardinal metric may be artificially aggregated through factor analysis to produce an attribute of enhanced
suitability for choice-set representation. Aggregating "factor structures" obtained from participants in the stock market study are
shown in Appendix C. In my view, they represent a significant
advance in our understanding of how stock market participants
vary in their thinking.

7. The reasons for proceeding as I did are noted in Chapter 4.

# 6

**Measuring Market Participant Assumptions — Algorithmic Estimation**

In the preceding chapter, factor analysis was used to construct a kind of attribute factor space. This space is peculiar to each subject; within it he can be viewed as construing the choice alternatives. Each attribute factor represents an economical way of characterizing the distinctions among alternatives. In this chapter, we demonstrate a procedure for estimating relationships between the position of alternatives in this space and the decision-maker's preferences. Again, much of the discussion is of a mildly technical nature and requires familiarity with empirical use of statistics for its appreciation. These parts may be omitted at first reading but should be mastered if the reader hopes to apply the method himself in small-sample circumstances.

The background aim of this study of stock market participants was concerned not principally with the actual content of decision-makers' cognitive images of individual stocks, though this is of interest in its own right. Rather it was aimed at the development of generally applicable procedures for measuring assumptions. In keeping with this aim, the measurement procedure was made as algorithmic as practicable, to promote its objectivity and feasibility in practical use. Thus, if the models that result from the procedure described here hold up for new data, as described in the next chapter, it will be the *measurement procedure*, not only the particular models of assumptions, which will have been validated.

The plan of this chapter is to deal with the following topics: Questionnaires 2 and 3, some expected difficulties in statistical modeling, and the use of factor measures to condense the data. A summary of the whole procedure is given in Table 6.2, page 106.

Table 6.1
Stocks Used in Questionnaires 2 and 3

| | |
|---|---|
| 1. Anaconda | 11. Monsanto |
| 2. American Motors | 12. Loew's Theatres |
| 3. City Investing | 13. Pacific Petroleum, Ltd. |
| 4. Brunswick | 14. Magnavox |
| 5. Delta Air Lines | 15. Std. Oil of New Jersey |
| 6. Four Seasons Nursing Centers | 16. R.C.A. |
| 7. Fairchild Camera | 17. Amer. Mach. and Fndry. |
| 8. Dymo Industries | 18. Sperry Rand |
| 9. International Tel. and Tel. | 19. Varian Associates |
| 10. General Electric | 20. United Aircraft |

### 6.1. Questionnaires 2 and 3

In July 1969, Questionnaires 2 and 3 were mailed to the subjects. Questionnaire 2 was identical to Questionnaire 1 except for three aspects. First, raw attribute scales were individually predivided into the number of content-equivalence intervals used by the subject in Questionnaire 1. Second, a common list of twenty stocks was used by all subjects, so that more intersubject comparisons could be made. Third, an average of about fifteen percent of the attributes on Questionnaire 1 were omitted as superfluous. The common list of twenty stocks used for both Questionnaires 2 and 3 is shown in Table 6.1.[1]

Questionnaire 3, a facsimile of which is shown in Appendix B, gave each decision-maker an opportunity to rate the same common list of stocks along some particular investment objective. On the hypothesis that the subject could make much finer discriminations along this final preference scale than for most of the individ-

1. The procedure used in selecting these stocks depended on frequency of mention in the *Wall Street Transcript* and *The Value Line* and random chance.

ual raw attribute scales, this scale was predivided into twenty intervals.[2]

Questionnaires 2 and 3 were returned an average of about one month after the date of mailing, with a minimum of a few days and a maximum of two months. Thirty-two subjects, of the thirty-nine who had completed Questionnaire 1, successfully completed this step. About half of the subjects did not complete the questionnaires until reminded. This seemed to occur because of two main reasons.

First, the decision-makers still felt the questionnaires were too long for the reward they expected, the investigator's promise to furnish them with a model of themselves and each of the other participants.

Second, some decision-makers may not have been able to bring themselves to make a preference commitment against which their skill might later be evaluated.

Still, however, the subject responses were not bad considering the typical responses encountered in mailed questionnaire studies. This high rate of cooperation may possibly be attributed to the commitment induced by the earlier interview.

The procedure used for estimating models relating stock attributes to preferences was fundamentally standard least-squares multiple regression. The major modification was that raw data from Questionnaire 2 were transformed into quasi factor measure data before being used as explanatory variables in regression equations. The dependent variable was the list of preference ratings from Questionnaire 3. The ratings of Questionnaire 3 were coded from 0 to 1000, as for the attribute data, but no allowance was

2. Other data gathered in Questionnaire 2 included expectations for twelve-month price increases. These data have never been analyzed.

made for special codes. The reader should note the example Questionnaire 3 responses shown in Appendix B. A few subjects omitted one or more of the stocks on Questionnaire 3; these cases were omitted before regression models were estimated.

## 6.2. Some Expected Difficulties in Statistical Modeling[3]

The author was previously advised by colleagues not to expect success in this modeling attempt. One, a behavioral scientist in the Simon-Clarkson tradition, was extremely skeptical of the prospect of modeling decision-makers using any kind of statistical estimation. He was of the opinion that the only really practical approach was to get a direct decision-net model through introspective protocol data from the decision-maker as he actually went through the mental steps of the decision. He also opined that "weights" models of the type which would result from simple multiple regression, as opposed to sequential decision trees, were discredited as models of the way decision-makers really make decisions. The second source, a labor economist, was skeptical on the basis of economists' experience in attempting to predict individual behavior, as opposed to group averages. He thought it was just "extremely difficult to find good explanatory variables for predicting individual behavior."[4] It is apparent after the experience of the stock market research that both these views have considerable merit, but are perhaps too pessimistic, as the reader may judge for himself.

The first and most obvious difficulty in regression modeling, utilizing the data available from Questionnaires 2 and 3, is that there are simply too many potential explanatory variables (20 to

3. This section may be omitted by the reader not overly interested in the detailed rationale of the statistical methods.
4. These are personal communications from M. Lavin, M.I.T., and R. Freeman, University of Chicago.

40) and too few observations (20) for each subject. However, if one hypothesizes that most human decisions are made utilizing quite limited cognitive facilities with respect to calculations involving large numbers of variables, one begins to suspect that major aspects of preference decisions are made utilizing only a few variables which somehow represent most of the relevant information.[5] Also, even a casual inspection of the Questionnaire 2 data reveals considerable informational redundancy. For example, one particular subject will usually rate companies having a "high 5-year profit growth rate" as having also "good management," and so it goes. This suggests that economies may be realized by finding ways to transform the data so that information (in the Shannon sense) is compacted into a few explanatory variables. Whether such a transformation is one that the decision-makers themselves ever explicitly undertake is not investigated; what is important here is whether the outside observer can fruitfully make such a transformation in his choice-set representation.

A factor analysis of the data followed by regression of the dependent variable against the resulting factor scores suggests itself for this reason. In addition, factor scores, being linear aggregations, have the desirable property of typically representing more cardinal metric information than any of the individual raw data attributes which contribute to them, as noted in the previous chapter.

Furthermore, the factor scores, being uncorrelated with each other, may allow one to eliminate the very serious problem in empirical research of multicollinearity between explanatory variables in running the regressions (Johnston 1963).

Use of factor scores for these purposes as typically practiced,

5. See Miller (1967), especially the essay on "the magical number seven."

however, may not be tenable.[6] There is a severe difficulty connected with regression of a dependent variable against factor
scores derived from a factor analysis based on the same data. It is
well known that the observed squared multiple correlation of a
dependent variable with any least-squares estimate based on the
independent variables is not an unbiased estimator; it is biased
upward from the true population squared multiple correlation coefficient. Now, the smaller the sample and also the larger the
number of explanatory variables, the greater the expected extent
of this explanatory inflation (Fisher 1928). Thus, on the average
one may expect a regression model to perform worse on fresh data
than on the data from which it is estimated. The extent of this
expected degradation is measured by the aforementioned bias.
Now what kind of bias can we expect utilizing factor scores for
regression? It is clear that population multicollinearity in the explanatory variables reduces the number of effectively distinct independent explanatory variables and thus the potential bias. Regression using population factor scores would be, thus, highly desirable. However, in real-world estimating, the factor scores, and
more pertinently the factor structure itself, are sample observations, not true underlying population values. Here lies the difficulty — the same kind of bias which inflates the squared multiple
correlation coefficient in regression works to inflate the observed
eigenvalues of the factors we estimate in factor analysis. Again, the
smaller the sample, the worse the bias. Thus, if we perform a

6. This paragraph was written before Herzberg's (1969) partly contradicting
result discussed in Section 4.1. He showed that factor scores based on a factor
analysis of the same data produced more reliable prediction equations than
did the larger number of original variables. The reader may still find the
reasoning of interest, however. The issue raised is yet unresolved, to my best
knowledge.

regression of the dependent variable on factor scores based on a factor analysis of the same data, the implied condensation of the data is at least partly, and perhaps totally, illusory.[7]

On the other hand, if we apply an a priori transformation to the data to reduce it to a few variables, the reduction in the expected inflation of explanatory power of the resulting regression models is not illusory. Where does one get the a priori knowledge required? This knowledge can be derived from a factor analysis of some different data sample taken from the same multivariate population. This step represents a mildly innovational departure from usual practice.[8]

### 6.3. Use of Factor Measures to Condense the Data

The data from Questionnaire 1 were factor analyzed in order to derive a transform that could then be applied to fresh data from succeeding questionnaires. Since the estimated factor structure was itself a small-sample observation, the resulting transform was imperfect compared to that which might be derivable from the population factor structure. However, the knowledge thus brought to bear, though imperfect, was distinctly useful. By allowing a reduction of the number of explanatory variables, it made possible regression models upon which one could place some confidence. A maximum of ten factor measures was to be used in regression models based on twenty observations.[9]

7. It is clear from Herzberg's result that the condensation is not *totally* illusory in most practical cases.
8. The other advantages of this practice were discussed in Section 4.1.
9. Unless otherwise noted, "factor measure" subsequently refers only to variables derived from data using a transform based on a factor structure itself estimated from another data set. A maximum of ten rotated factors were derived for each subject, as described earlier.

The derivation of the transforms is expressed mathematically in Appendix A and follows Harmon (1967). This transform gives us the $\alpha_{kj}$ coefficients mentioned on page 79 of the previous chapter. Its calculation requires knowledge only of the factor loadings and eigenvalues of the original factor analysis of Questionnaire 1 data. It was in practice calculated by a modification of the factor analysis program that I used.[10] The algorithm requires only simple matrix multiplication and transposition.

The transformation might be applied either to $Z$, the normalized raw attribute data, or to $X$, the nonnormalized raw data.[11] However, if applied to $Z$, changes in the mean or in the variance of the raw attribute data would not be reflected in changes in the factor measures. This reflection was thought to be desirable in order to make convenient any study of shifts through time in the attribute or preference scale properties. Therefore, the transforms were applied directly to the raw attribute data of Questionnaire 2 to derive nonnormalized factor measures, which are hereafter referred to simply as "factor measures." This use of the transform on the nonnormalized raw data mildly disturbed the orthogonality of the factor measures and is not necessarily recommended generally.

## 6.4. A Significance Test for Factors[12]

The condensation of the explanatory variables achievable through the foregoing transform procedure made small-sample regression

10. This was the BioMed package. See Dixon (1968). For further details, see Appendix A.
11. $Z_{ij} = (X_{ij} - \overline{X}_j)/\hat{\sigma}(X_j)$.
12. This section may be omitted without loss of continuity by the reader uninterested in statistical method.

feasible. However, I was still concerned with increasing the available degrees of freedom in the regressions. Therefore, a test of significance for rotated factor eigenvalues in the original Questionnaire 1 data was made, and only "significant" factor measures as defined by this test were used as explanatory variables in the regressions. This reduced the number of potential explanatory variables for each subject to an integer between 1 and 7, depending on the subject. The derivation of the test is described in the following paragraphs.

I was not satisfied with the available statistical tests on the significance of factor eigenvalues; the theory of such tests had not been completely worked out in the statistical literature, even for the multivariate normal case (Sugiyama 1966). Even worse, most of the theory available did not appear particularly suitable for use with *rotated* factors. In order to obtain a useful test without having to derive the relevant sampling theory, one may conduct a Monte Carlo simulation with random data. The objective is to estimate empirically some of the sampling properties of the eigenvalues of the rotated factors when they are based on a random sample whose population eigenvalues are negligible. The use of pseudorandom data in the simulation made the resulting test even more conservative. The pseudorandom data were prepared by shuffling raw Questionnaire 1 data from six different subjects together and dividing the data arbitrarily into 15 data sets of 20 observations each. Of these, there were 5 sets with 15 variables, 5 sets with 30 variables, and 5 sets with 45 variables. These sets of data were factor analyzed according to the identical procedure used in factor analyzing Questionnaire 1, and the resulting eigenvalues for the rotated factors calculated.

Figures 6.1, 6.2, and 6.3 present the results of this Monte Carlo

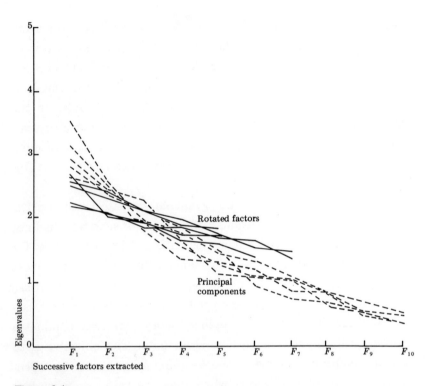

Figure 6.1
Monte Carlo Simulation of Factor Analysis, $n = 15$, $N = 20$

simulation analysis. The first chart, Figure 6.1, shows the sample distributions for the eigenvalues for the data set where the number of variables, $n$, was set equal to 15. It will be noted that the successive eigenvalues of the rotated factors are more even than those of the principal components, as might be expected. Also, as with the regular Questionnaire 1 data, different numbers of factors were rotated, depending on the sample covariance matrix.

In the second chart, Figure 6.2, data from all three subsets, $n = 15$, $n = 30$, and $n = 45$, were entered on one chart, whose

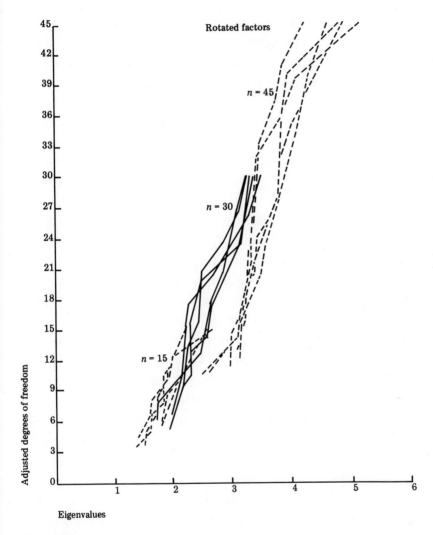

Figure 6.2
Monte Carlo Eigenvalues Plotted against Adjusted Degrees of Freedom

coordinates differ from the first. The ordinate and abscissa have been reversed, and the eigenvalues are plotted against a quantity labeled "adjusted degrees of freedom" rather than successive factors extracted. The "adjusted degrees of freedom" quantity is obtained by cumulatively subtracting from the original number of explanatory variables the eigenvalues of the factors previously extracted. The most important feature on the chart is that the transformation to "adjusted degrees of freedom" has produced near-linear functional invariance between eigenvalues and adjusted degrees of freedom.

The importance of this point is that it makes feasible a relatively simple combination of the $n = 15$ and $n = 30$ cases, say, to derive tests of significance for the case of, say, $n = 22$.

The third chart, Figure 6.3, shows the test that was constructed by linearly estimating (except that the line was broken into two segments for $n = 45$) the expected values $\overline{E}$ of the eigenvalues $E$ from the second chart, and separately estimating the standard deviation as a linear function of the adjusted degrees of freedom. A test line derived from the Tchebycheff inequality was drawn at three estimated standard deviations from the mean, for each of the three cases, $n = 15$, 30, and 45. In using the derived test, intermediate cases such as that for $n = 22$ were tested with reference to a test line drawn at $(22 - 25)/(30 - 15)$ of the distance from the $n = 15$ test line to the $n = 30$ test line.

No claim is made that the resulting test is equivalent to one that might one day be derived from theory. However, it appears to be a useful, conservative heuristic. A major point in its favor is that it furnishes a way in which algorithmic, objective selection of a subset of the factor measures can be made. This effectively counters one of the major objections to the use of factor analysis, the

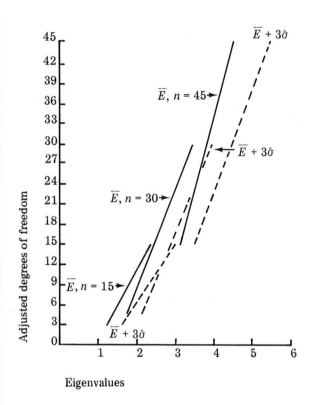

Eigenvalues

Figure 6.3
Monte Carlo Derived Test for Factor Significance

subjectivity typically implicit in deciding when to stop factoring. As such, this kind of test represents a considerable innovation from widespread practice in factor analysis. The results of this significance test were utilized in selecting the subset of attribute factors for each decision-maker reported in Appendix C.

### 6.5. A Robust Test to Reject Explanatory Variables from Regression Models[13]

The BMD stepwise regression computation package (Dixon 1968) was used in the regression of the preference data of Questionnaire 3 against the factor measures derived utilizing the foregoing procedures from Questionnaire 2. This BMD program has the desirable feature that the user can preselect the order of explanatory variables to be forced into the regression equation and still get the benefits of stepwise information as to successive multiple correlations with the dependent variable, partial correlations of variables not yet entered into the equation, and "$F$" (and thus "$t$") statistics on variables, both in and out of the equation. For each subject, a stepwise regression was run in which the previously tested "significant" factor measures were successively forced into the explanatory equation. The factors were made to enter into the equation in order of descending magnitude of eigenvalues until the last significant factor was included.

After analyzing the result of this computer estimation series, one had to make a decision as to which of these potential explanatory variables appeared to be useful predictors of the dependent

13. Again, this section may be omitted without loss of continuity by the reader uninterested in statistical refinements. Their major justification for appearing in this book is that they may be necessary when using small samples of observations.

variable. In order to avoid the necessity of subjective judgment particular to one's impression of each subject, an objective test was desirable for guiding the choice of the explanatory variables to be retained in the final regression equation.

The standard $F$-test (or similarly, $t$-tests) would have probably given adequate results here, given a priori rejection levels; however, a different test was developed, based on a test suggested by Linhart.[14]

The explanatory variables were clearly themselves partly random variables, which put into question the use of $F$-tests for determining best prediction equations. On the other hand, Linhart's proposed test assumes errors in variables in the normal multivariate case. It tests at the 5 percent significance level the hypothesis that leaving in a particular explanatory variable will produce a shorter 95 percent confidence interval for the dependent variable than would omitting it.

I used Linhart's model to construct a test at the 25 percent significance level of the hypothesis that the 95 percent confidence interval of the dependent variable would be shortened. This test was put in a convenient graphical form, as shown in Figure 6.4. It should be noted that the graph is specific to the case of twenty observations. Also, strictly speaking, it is properly applied only to the case where one single possible omission is selected a priori before the regression run. Its use in the procedure described in the following section makes it only an approximate test because these conditions are not precisely fulfilled. No claim is made here that the test is optimum, only that it is convenient.

Whether or not the $F$-test or the Linhart test had been used, the

14. See Linhart (1960), and also Johnston (1963).

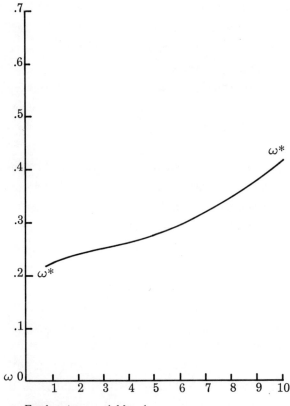

Explanatory variables, $k$

$N = 20$

$$\omega = \frac{R_k^2 - R_{k-1}^2}{1 - R_{k-1}^2}$$

Reject $k$th explanatory variable if $\omega < \omega^*$

Figure 6.4
Modified Linhart Test to Omit a Single Variable from a Regression

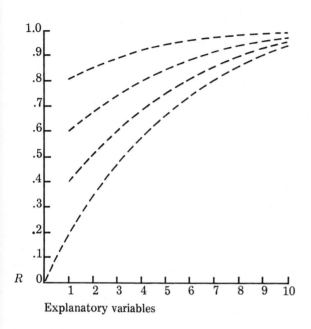

$R$

Explanatory variables

Figure 6.5
A Modified Linhart Test to Omit Variables Tentatively from a Stepwise
Forced Sequence, for the Case $N = 20$

most important point to stress again is that some such test provides an aid to algorithmic, objective choosing of a predictive model. It thus leads to a more objective, and because it requires less
subjective skill, a more feasible measure of decision assumptions.

The formula of Figure 6.4 was transformed into the more convenient form shown in Figure 6.5. The latter shows for a stepwise
regression the sequence $R_k^2$ values required to keep an explanatory
variable from being rejected. It is an approximation of Figure 6.4.

## 6.6. Obtaining Predictive Regression Models
The only information readily accessible as to *decrements* in $R^2$
with the dependent variable as one independent variable at a time

Table 6.2

An Algorithm for Measuring Decision Assumptions
___

START

1. Collect and code Questionnaire 1 data.

2. Conduct factor analysis.

3. Calculate transforms necessary for factor measure calculation (use step 2).

4. Calculate eigenvalues of rotated factors (use step 2).

5. Collect and code Questionnaires 2 and 3.

6. Apply transform (from step 3) and data from Questionnaire 2 (from step 5) to calculate factor measures.

7. Test significance of factors. Reject factor measures whose associated factors tested insignificant (use step 4).

8. Estimate stepwise regression equations explaining the Questionnaire 3 data ($Y$) on the basis of the factor measures ($F_k$) remaining after step 7. Force the $F_k$ into the stepwise regression in *descending* order of magnitude of the eigenvalues obtained in step 4.

9. Tentatively reject explanatory variables not passing the modified Linhart test applied sequentially.

10A. If no explanatory variables remain, force in $F_k$ with the highest correlation with $Y$.

10B. Otherwise, model according to the best predictive algorithm described in Table 6.3.

11A. If $F_k$ is not the factor measure associated with the largest eigenvalue, force in the latter also.

11B. END

12. END
___

was eliminated from the full set of explanatory variables were the *increments* in $R^2$ produced by the stepwise regression procedure at each step. Therefore, the test could only be used to test the inclusion of a variable in the set of variables *thus far* forced into the regression equation. Usually, this seemed fairly adequate; the factor measures were typically not highly correlated with each other, because they were based on orthogonal factor structure derived from data in Questionnaire 1. Also, the order of forcing produced results confirming my a priori supposition that the more important explanatory variables correspond, in general, to factors with large eigenvalues. However, because of this approximation, some further search for the best predictive model was sometimes occasioned. This algorithmic search algorithm used is explained in the following paragraphs. A more precise description of it is given in Tables 6.2 and 6.3.

Table 6.3.

**A Subalgorithm for Choosing a Good Predictive Equation (Occasionally used for determining further "dress" runs)**

1. Rerun stepwise regression, omitting up to two of the factor measures tentatively rejected on the last step; if more than two were rejected, omit the two which were earliest in the forcing sequence.

2. Check to see if the second of the two omitted variables, if any, has a higher partial correlation with $Y$ than the remaining included variables which now pass the Linhart test at any point in the stepwise regression. If so, rerun the regression, bringing back this omitted variable and including it in its previous place in the sequence.

3. Tentatively reject any remaining explanatory variables not passing the Linhart test sequentially. If any variables are rejected at this point, go back to step 1. If none are rejected, go to step 4.

4. If the model's $R^2$ can be improved by adding one already rejected variable whose addition reduces the $t$-value of an already accepted variable below 1.0, do so and rerun the regression, omitting the low $t$-valued variable.

5. Return to step 11B of the main algorithm in Table 6.2.

Sample results using the algorithm are shown in Figure 6.6. The dotted lines represent test lines, the solid line the results of the stepwise regression for Subject 30. The first two explanatory variables whose additional $R^2$ causes the slope of the actual result line to be less steep than the slope of nearby test lines were tentatively omitted.

On the second round of stepwise regression runs, one or more "dress runs" with fewer variables were carried out. Typically, only one dress run was conducted, but if there were too many tentatively omitted variables, additional runs were made to explore the intermediate space. In the test for Subject 30, shown in Figure 6.6, the decision was made more complex by the fact that the "$t$" statistic's value for the factor attribute $F_1$ was reduced below 1.0 by the addition of $F_4$ and $F_5$. In such cases, also, a second dress run was conducted. This "refinement" I later judged to have been unwise.

In a few cases, no explanatory variables passed the test; there, the most statistically significant factor was forced into the dress run regression equation. If different, the factor measure with the largest eigenvalue was also forced into the equation. Parenthetically, the fact that in many of these apparent-failure cases the model thus estimated was later validated indicates that the a priori reliance on factors with large eigenvalues was well placed. The reason the $t$-test "refinement" was later judged to have been unwise was because it operated counter to this largest-eigenvalue heuristic.

In the foregoing manner, regression models relating the attribute factor measures to the decision-maker's preference ratings were estimated. Many such models are shown in Appendix D.[15]

15. Together with Appendix C, they probably represent the largest and most detailed existing body of descriptive data relevant to decision assumptions of stock market participants.

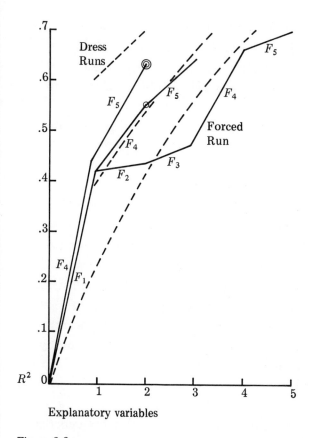

Figure 6.6
Explained Variance by Stepwise Forced Sequence Regression, Subject 30,
$N = 20$.

Again, the reader is advised that I now judge that step 4 of the subalgorithm in Table 6.3 was a mistake. It runs counter to a heuristic shown very effective by the validation results of the study — when in doubt, choose the attribute factor with the largest eigenvalue.

The form of the resulting assumption models is illustrated by that for Subject 19:

$$Y = 1690 - (1.54)F_1 - (0.78)F_4.$$

That is, the preference code $Y$ is predicted. It is measured as a function of attribute factors whose loadings with respect to raw attributes were illustrated in Chapter 5, p. 86. This decision-maker is represented as assuming that the stocks of companies which he views as serving rapidly growing markets and having sophisticated, innovative management are better investments ($F_1$). He also appears to assume that stocks whose price has risen recently are better investments ($F_4$). These particular assumptions are by no means common to all market participants.

## In Summary

In many managerial decision situations, the number of apparently pertinent raw attributes is large. On the other hand, the manager's time is valuable. Also, the number of decisions from which it is possible to take observations may be small. Thus, the observations obtainable are few and the models of decision assumptions to be estimated are many. The result is typically a severe shortage of available degrees of freedom. In fact, in the study of stock market participants, I was usually faced with more attributes than observations.

These problems force upon the prospective measurer numerous

small sophistications unnecessary for larger data samples. First, the factor structures estimated in the previous chapter are used to transform the raw attribute data to a much smaller number of nearly orthogonal attribute factors. Of these, only those factors with statistically significant eigenvalues are used as candidates for regression. Then these new independent variables are entered into a step-wise regression in descending order of eigenvalues, using a stringent test of regression significance to prevent searching effects.

The equations thus estimated in the stock market participant study are shown in Appendix D. They may be interpreted with the aid of the factor structures in Appendix C.

Measuring Market Participant
Assumptions — Predictive
Validation

## 7.1. The Method Completed

In Chapter 5, the origin of attribute factor measures was described. In Chapter 6 the procedure used to model their relationship with preference data was presented. This relationship is a
measure of the assumptions underlying decisions. In the present
chapter the validation of the resulting models in the study of stock
market participants is described. Such validation procedures are an
integral part of the method.

Let us continue the description of the study of stock market
participants. In September 1969, Questionnaires 4 and 5 were
mailed to the subjects. These were essentially identical to Questionnaires 2 and 3. Twenty-five subjects, out of thirty-two to
whom they were mailed, returned them completed. In general, the
average quality of the questionnaires returned, in terms of apparent care with which they were filled out, seemed noticeably better
than the average quality of Questionnaires 2 and 3.

The participation by subjects in the study is shown in Table 7.1.
Subject withdrawals from the study appear to have been influenced by job change, withdrawal of social support, and work load
imposed by the questionnaire. This conclusion is the result of a
least-squares regression of the dependent dummy variable "withdrawal" against surrogates for these variables. Job change was
taken as unity if the subject left the financial organization through
which he was initially contacted and in which there were other
subjects participating in the study, zero otherwise. Withdrawal of
social support was defined as the percentage of subjects in his
organization who had failed to complete a previous questionnaire.
The work-load measure was the number of raw attribute scales on
the subject's questionnaire. Other interpretations of the meaning
of these measures are possible, but in any case they collectively

explain about twenty-five percent of the variance in subject with-drawal from the study, where subject withdrawal is taken as unity and subject participation through Questionnaire 5 as zero.

The stocks rated by the subjects in Questionnaires 4 and 5 included 10 stocks used previously and 10 stocks that, though selected similarly, were different. They are listed together in Table 7.2.

The data from Questionnaires 4 and 5 were coded using the method applied to Questionnaires 2 and 3. The raw attribute data

Table 7.1.
Participation in Each Stage of the Study

| Stage | Number of Subjects Completed |
| --- | --- |
| Interview | 40 |
| Questionnaire 1 | 39 |
| Questionnaire 2 | 33 |
| Questionnaire 3 | 32 |
| Questionnaire 4 | 25 |
| Questionnaire 5 | 25 |

Table 7.2.
Stocks Used in Questionnaires 4 and 5

| | |
| --- | --- |
| 1.  American Machinery and Foundry | 11. LTV |
| 2.  Bethlehem Steel | 12. Massey-Ferguson |
| 3.  Chrysler | 13. Monsanto |
| 4.  City Investing | 14. Pacific Petroleum |
| 5.  Control Data | 15. Polaroid |
| 6.  Delta Airlines | 16. Simon & Schuster |
| 7.  Digital Equipment | 17. Standard Oil (Ind.) |
| 8.  Fairchild Camera | 18. Standard Oil (N.J.) |
| 9.  Four Seasons N.C. | 19. Texas Instruments |
| 10. Int'l Tel. and Tel. | 20. Varian Associates |

were transformed into attribute factor measures using the transforms obtained earlier from the original Questionnaire 1 factor
structure.

The validation test was as follows. The previously estimated
regression model was applied to the Questionnaire 4 factor measures to derive a predictor variable for the dependent preference
data of Questionnaire 5. The correlation coefficient between the
predictor variable and the dependent preference data was calculated. If the squared correlation coefficient exceeded that required
for acceptance by the modified Linhart test described earlier, and
if, in addition, the correlation coefficient was positive ($R > 0$), the
model was accepted as validated. In practice, this meant for $N$ =
20, $R^2 \geqslant .22$ and $R > 0$. In two cases where $N < 20$, the test was
adjusted accordingly. This combined test is equivalent in severity
to an $F$-test rejecting the hypothesis $R = 0$ at approximately the
1.5 percent level of significance ("one-tailed" equivalent). These
validation results are summarized in Table 7.3.

As can be seen in the table, the models of twenty of the twenty-
five remaining subjects appeared to be of some value. The models
were based on the measurement algorithm described in the previous chapter. Some of the subjects who initially seemed poorly
modeled were more predictable in the validation sample. An explanation is offered in Section 7.2. Five subjects represented complete failures. Again, the differences between characteristics of
these cases and the main body are summarized in Section 7.2. The
following comments represent my subjective impressions.

The main distinguishing features of the five failures were one or
more of the following. They were out of touch with stock market
conditions, as measured by a preponderance of special codes 501
and 502 in the raw attribute data. They were young, individual

Table 7.3.
Assumption Estimation and Validation Results

| Subject | Quest. 2 and 3, $R_e{}^2$ | Quest. 4 and 5, $R_v{}^2$ | Result | Comments |
|---|---|---|---|---|
| 01 | .29 | .60 | val. | |
| 03 | .51 | .25 | n.val. | $R < 0$ |
| 04 | .56 | .26 | val. | |
| 05 | .27 | .36 | val. | |
| 07 | .52 | .67 | val. | |
| 13 | .10 | .65 | val. | |
| 14 | .29 | .03 | n.val. | |
| 15 | .78 | .39 | val. | |
| 16 | .04 | .41 | val. | |
| 17 | .60 | .25 | val. | |
| 19 | .82 | .63 | val. | |
| 20 | .39 | .35 | val. | |
| 21 | .07 | .05 | n.val. | |
| 22 | .60 | .61 | val. | |
| 23 | .12 | .00 | n.val. | |
| 24 | .60 | .35 | val. | |
| 26 | .59 | .68 | val. | |
| 27 | .29 | .34 | val. | |
| 28 | .50 | .45 | val. | |
| 30 | .63 | .29 | val. | |
| 31 | .12 | .60 | val. | |
| 35 | .64 | .37 | val. | |
| 37 | .02 | .47 | val. | |
| 38 | .20 | .44 | val. | |
| 39 | .19 | .05 | n.val. | |

investors with relatively little investing experience. Or, in Questionnaire 3 they appeared to favor the "defensive" pole of an attribute factor characterizable as "defensive" versus "aggressive" stocks. Their responses to Questionnaire 5 were made in the midst of a substantial general rise in the stock market. At that point, "defensive" stocks fell out of their favor. Such a tactic could not be modeled because attributes of markets (as opposed to attributes of stocks) were not measured. Thus, assumptions dependent on the particular time phase of the stock market as a whole tended to cause difficulty, especially where the time interval between questionnaires was long.

Taking into account both successes and failures, was the method for measuring decision assumptions found useful? Under plausible assumptions, the null hypothesis that the models are of no predictive value was certainly rejected. The binomial expectation of finding 20 or more out of 25 cases validated at the .015 level of significance is infinitesimal.[1] The average variance explained in the validation test is a little over 38 percent.

There is a disquieting possibility. Perhaps these "validation" results were spurious. The validated assumptions might just have been associates of the specific, unmeasured attribute features of the ten stocks used in both the estimating questionnaires and the validating questionnaires. Even though new responses had been gathered from the decision-makers, there would still be a tendency toward reproduction of the original ordering of the ten stocks. To test this possibility, the validation of the measure was redone,

---

1. The precise joint significance level depends on the adequacy of the normality assumption. Spot checks reveal no significant departures of the residuals from a normal distribution. However, even a nonparametric sign test would have yielded joint significance at the $2^{-20}$ level.

using only the remaining ten stocks in Questionnaires 4 and 5
which had *not* appeared earlier. For these totally new stocks, the
average explanatory power of the predictive equation for the new
preference ratings was $R^2 = .31$. The reduction in $R^2$ from .38 to
.31 is clearly significant.

Thus, the disquieting suspicion appears well founded. However, even when it is accounted for, there remains a core of
predictive ability. Therefore the models and the method are still
validated.

What about the practicality of the method? Many of the participants were mutual fund portfolio managers, security analysts,
bank investment officers, and trust officers. The original Role
Repertory Test took, in this case, an average of less than an hour.
The ratings used for factor analysis and regression were done using
mailed questionnaires, but reports indicate less than two hours,
probably only an hour, was spent on average for each of these. In
all, the average time spent by the decision-maker to get the measure was probably no more than four hours. The data collection
and statistical analysis, indeed the entire procedure, is otherwise
mostly susceptible to computerization and can be done at this
scale very economically. Given the objectivity of the results, and
the low level of skill required of the measurer to enter the data
into the analysis, the methodology seems to perform very favorably as compared to other methods, if practical feasibility is the
criterion of choice. However, decisive comparisons obviously await
further experimentation.

What do these results imply? It has been demonstrated that it is
possible to measure practically a substantial relationship between a
decision-maker's image of the raw attributes of a choice alternative
and his preferences. Thus, his assumptions are modeled. This was

done using what might be termed algorithmic regression techniques and even with relatively small samples of observations. Thus, the measure appears both objective and feasible.

The resulting models are not overwhelming in explanatory or predictive power; they do, however, establish a reasonable basis for progress. Furthermore, even these simple models capture enough of the decision-makers' assumptions to be useful in managerial planning and control. Useful applications are described in Chapters 9 and 10.

## 7.2. Additional Validation Analysis[2]

Of the twenty-five decision-makers who completed Questionnaire 5, twenty proved sufficiently predictable through the methods described earlier to pass the model validation test described in the previous section. The question naturally arises as to whether one could have predicted on the basis of earlier data whether the assumption measures of a particular subject would be validated. This question is associated with the more general question of whether there exist early clues as to the final correlation between the actual and predicted preference data of Questionnaire 5.

A related issue is raised when one observes the changes in the $R^2$ of the model from the estimation data ($R_e^{\,2}$) to the validation data ($R_v^{\,2}$). Several sharp *increases* occurred. The most dramatic was from $R_e^{\,2} = .12$ to $R_v^{\,2} = .65$. A few such increases might be expected, but can a larger number of such increases be explained or predicted?

One can separate the determinants of ultimate validation into two parts:

2. This section can be omitted without loss of continuity. The reader who is interested in improving the technology of measurement further may find it of interest, however.

1. $R_e{}^2$ resulting from model estimation,
2. change between $R_e{}^2$ and $R_v{}^2$.

A plausible determinant of $R_e{}^2$ which was easy to check was the subject's **unfamiliarity** with, and inattention to, the stocks used in Questionnaires 2 and 3. This was expected to have a negative effect. For **unfamiliarity** $U$ the total number of the subject's "not enough information" responses on Questionnaire 2 was divided by the number of raw attributes he used. In addition, $R_e{}^2$ tends to be an increasing function of $K$, the number of explanatory variables in the model. Regression analysis of the measures $U$ and $K$ as predictors of $R_e{}^2$ showed strong effects in the expected direction. Other major determinants of $R_e{}^2$ are, of course, the adequacy of the choice representation approach, the investigator's skill in eliciting raw attribute labels, small-sample error in the original factor analysis, and the stability of the factor structure between Questionnaire 1 and Questionnaire 2.

## 7.3. The Model's Validation Adequacy

One would expect the change in $R^2$ between $R_e{}^2$ and $R_v{}^2$ to be a function of four influences. The first is a negative influence of the time span between questionnaires. The second is a negative influence of instability of the subject's conceptual structure. The third is a negative influence of the number of explanatory variables in the estimated model. Finally, the fourth is a positive influence caused by the inclusion of valid a priori information in the estimated model. The following measures were thought to be at least moderately associated with the foregoing variables. For the **time span** $T$ we used the days elapsed between filling out Questionnaires 3 and 5. For the measure of instability $I$ we used whether or not the subject was a member of a financial institution or was a private investor:

$$I = \begin{cases} 1, \text{ if private investor,} \\ 0, \text{ otherwise} \end{cases}$$

Of course, aspects of age and experience would have been better measures for this variable. The number of explanatory variables, $K$, on which $R_e{}^2$ is based was given. Finally, the measure of a priori information depended on whether or not the investigator had forced into the regression model the factor measure with the largest eigenvalue in the last step of the modeling process described in Chapter 6. This was done whenever no explanatory variable passed the modified Linhart test and the explanatory variable having the greatest correlation with the dependent variable was not the factor measure with the largest eigenvalue. A priori information $A$ was defined as

$$A = \begin{cases} 1, \text{ if } F_{E \text{ max}} \text{ added to statistically ``best'' model,} \\ 0, \text{ otherwise.} \end{cases}$$

Parenthetically, $A = 1$ for three subjects, Subjects 16, 27, and 38.

The following results were obtained for a stepwise regression in which the sequence of entering variables was prespecified, where $y$ = $100\,(R_v{}^2 - R_e{}^2), N = 25$:

| | |
|---|---|
| $y = 39 - T(0.65)$, | $R^2 = .11$ |
| $y = 39 - T(0.65) + I(0.27)$, | $R^2 = .11$ |
| $y = 37 - T(0.66) + K(2.1) - I(0.05)$, | $R^2 = .11$ |
| $y = 24 - T(0.28) - K(9.4) - I(0.57) + A(41)$, | $R^2 = .28.$ |

The $t^2$ values appropriate to each of the coefficients are given in the following table:

| T   | K   | I   | A   |
|-----|-----|-----|-----|
| 2.7 |     |     |     |
| 2.6 |     | 0.0 |     |
| 2.5 | 0.0 | 0.0 |     |
| 0.5 | 0.6 | 0.0 | 4.8 |

We see that only time span $T$ and a priori information $A$ seem to have any marked influence on the change in $R^2$ between $R_e{}^2$ and $R_v{}^2$. Their influence is highly collinear. That is, increased time generally has a negative effect, but this is countered in the cases where a priori information was added. The implication is that the factors with large eigenvalues are much more likely to relate to enduring assumptions which may have been temporarily diverted at the time of measurement. Again, there is otherwise some weak evidence that we may expect validation to become less likely with increased time span, although the estimated rate of decline is slow. In addition, it appears probable that the model estimation process could be improved through a more systematic addition of a priori information. The question of whether the measurement procedure influenced the decision-maker toward greater than normal consistency might be interesting to explore in a future study. However, in this study the time intervals were long enough to make it unlikely that the subject could remember his previous raw attribute responses.

### In Summary

In the preceding two chapters, we saw how to obtain a measurement of an individual's decision assumptions. How good are such measures? To find out, one needs to test the models thus obtained. This is done by correlating actual preferences according to new data with predicted preferences obtained by using the models to transform raw attribute ratings, being careful to include some really new alternatives.

In the stock market participant study, the previously estimated models of decision assumptions accounted, on average, for only about a third of the individual's variance in preference ratings. This average explanatory power is quite modest, but includes some cases of outright failure and some of great success. In my opinion, it is sufficient for useful applications in stock market decision-making.

As more experience is gained, one would expect two kinds of improvement in reliability. First, better measures may be gotten — for example, through collecting preference data at the time of the role repertory test. Second, it may prove practicable to predict those decision-makers and decisions that are especially susceptible to valid measurement, and to concentrate on these applications.

# 8

Comparison with Other
Decision Models of Stock
Market Participants

In this brief chapter we compare the measurement method described in the last four chapters with alternatives. Several other decision modeling methods have been used in the stock market context. Three of these are summarized here. The work by Slovic, by Green and Maheshwari, and by Clarkson are compared with that described in this book.

## 8.1. Choice-Set Representation—Analysis of Variance

Paul Slovic has done some interesting work in modeling the decision assumptions of two stockbrokers (Slovic 1969). His method consisted of the following steps. First, he discussed at some length with one of the stockbrokers the information sources he used. He concluded that all, or almost all, of this information could be represented by eleven items of data regarding individual stocks found in a well-known investment advisory publication.[1] He regarded each of these items as a dichotomous variable which took either "high" or "low" as its value. Next, he constructed artificial examples of stocks having various combinations of "high" and "low" associated with the eleven variables. He included sufficient examples (128) to estimate all the direct effects and effects of interactions of the variables taken two at a time. Higher-order interaction effects were not estimated. The main and two-way interaction effects were estimated on the basis of preference ratings of the 128 stocks on a nine-point scale. The two decision-makers were each given 128 standardized descriptions of these

---

1. These were attributes such as yield, "resistance level," past year's performance, and number of shares outstanding. The 128 observations in his experiment were required to give a 1/16 replication of the 2048 observations necessary to estimate all the higher-order interaction effects.

"unknown" stocks and asked to rate them on the nine-point preference scale. They reported spending about ten hours each on the
task.

Slovic's analysis of the resulting data explained 72 to 80 percent
of the variance by main effects and a small, but still significant
proportion, 5 to 7 percent, by interaction effects. The explanation
of variance is clearly highly significant.

Another finding of some interest was that neither decision-
maker appeared typically to use much more than half of the available attributes.

Slovic arrived at two major conclusions. First, his method yielded insights into the decision-making process which might be useful
to the decision-maker himself or to trainees for the same task.
Second, what he called configural processing (nonlinear interactions of attribute information) was apparently a part of the decision, because he did find significant two-variable interaction effects.

Both his work and that presented in this book use a choice-set
representation of decision assumptions. Another similarity is the
use of an artificially constructed task to arouse the activity of the
decision procedure to be modeled.

There is, however, a fundamental difference in methodology.
Slovic's method does not address the problem of initially eliciting
the attributes relevant to the decision. Slovic apparently does not
view this problem as difficult or worth a formal attack. There is no
way to judge from his results whether he included too few relevant
attributes. That is, his method provides no corrective signals when
too few relevant attributes have been included. This is because he
utilizes artificial alternatives which do not correspond to known
real alternatives. The decision-maker knows nothing about the arti-

ficial alternatives except the eleven attributes in terms of which Slovic presents them. Therefore, it is not surprising that the decision-maker's preferences are highly correlated with these attributes. One wonders what would happen if Slovic were to now test his model on real-world alternatives known to the decision-maker along other attributes. A sharp reduction of the explanatory power of the model would provide a signal of possible misspecification of the relevant attributes.

In consequence of this difficulty, we do not know how good Slovic's model would be even for the experimental situation studied by the author in which the decision was similarly artificial but the alternatives real.

What we can learn, however, is something of the potential gain we may obtain in model effectiveness by including nonlinear combinations of attributes (two-variable interaction effects) as explanatory variables for preferences.

## 8.2. Choice-Set Description — Multidimensional Scaling

Paul Green and Arun Maheshwari have applied multidimensional scaling (MDS) techniques to learning something about decision assumptions regarding common stocks.[2]

Their method was as follows. Using about twenty graduate students at a time as subjects, they collected data on perceived interstock similarities from each subject. They used ten real stocks as alternatives, and had each subject rank order the forty-five possible pairs in terms of similarity. The time required was not reported. These data were pooled across the group of students. Then they were analyzed by a nonmetric MDS technique. The resulting spatial configuration provided, according to Green, "an excellent

2. See Green and Maheshwari (1969).

fit" in two dimensions. It represented an aggregate of the different subjects' perceptual spaces. The two dimensions in this aggregated attribute space appeared to be associated with perceived risk and perceived return as measured by other means.

Each subject marked preference ratings for each stock on a seven-point scale. The experimenters then modeled decision assumptions by one of two methods, regression or specification of an ideal point. In regression, the previously obtained pooled data regarding the stock's joint position on each of the two aggregate dimensions were regressed against individual preference data. In the second method, a computer algorithm estimated ideal positive or ideal negative points in relation to the configuration of alternative stocks. It was supposed that preference was proportional to the square of the distance of the alternative from the ideal point. This procedure allows estimation of nonlinear indifference curves or, in Slovic's terms, configural decision rules.

Again, Green's method has several similarities with respect to the method of this book. An artificial decision task was used, but the alternatives were real. Second, the problem of eliciting the relevant attributes to the decision was specifically addressed. One gets the impression that the time required of the decision-maker was short. Another strong similarity in approach is his use of canonical correlations to relate configuration dimensions to more understandable attributes.

However, there are dramatic differences between Green and Maheshwari's method and that of this book. First, there is their use of multidimensional scaling. The MDS requirement of comparing all possible pairwise combinations of alternatives imposes a work load which rises nearly as the square of the number of alternatives considered. Thus, they were able to use only ten stocks as stimuli.

In addition the pooling of inhomogeneous attribute data created difficulties acknowledged by Green and Maheshwari in modeling the relation with preferences. It is not clear, for example, that two dimensions are adequate to describe the implied attributes inherent in the individual, as apposed to the aggregate, pooled ranking of similarities.

Further, their subjects were not real participants in the stock market. I, on the other hand, used active investors, security analysts, portfolio managers, etc.

In addition, Green and Maheshwari do not report the explanatory or predictive power of their models.

Finally, the difficulty in linking the two aggregate dimensions of the configurations constructed through MDS to interpretable decision inputs is significant. To be fair, Green and Maheshwari go a reasonable way toward solving this problem, however, in their use of canonical correlations.

## 8.3. Decision-Net Modeling

Probably the best-known model of decision-making in the stock market is that done by G. Clarkson of a single bank trust officer.[3] His approach is sharply different from those that depend on choice-set representation. It consists of a direct modeling of decision nets, which he calls discrimination nets. A decision process is represented as a sequence of decision nets operating on one alternative at a time. The input is a *list* of alternative stocks with an associated list of attribute properties for each alternative. The

3. See Clarkson (1962).

decision process is modeled as using one discrimination net at a time to transform a long list of stocks that are candidates for investment into a shorter list. A sequence of such discrimination net applications terminates when an appropriate portfolio, a short list of stocks satisfying certain requirements, has been constructed.

His empirical method consisted in close observation of a single trust officer over several months. Interviews alone proved unfruitful, so he resorted to observation of the trust officer as he made his work-related decisions. This was strategically combined with observation of artificially constructed decisions. The means of observation was the transcript of verbalized thought and actions of the decision-maker after instructing him to think or solve problems aloud. Its success depended on obtaining the subject's cooperation in verbalizing extremely detailed features of his thought process as it occurred.

The model that resulted was tested against actual work-related performance of the trust officer the next year. The test decision was the construction of a portfolio of from five to nine stocks out of a beginning list of eighty stocks. In each of four cases, the model selected all but one or two stocks correctly. This test is not directly comparable with tests of $R^2$ significance (which rely on a complete and cardinal preference ordering) used in this book. Clearly, however, it represents a high order of predictive power.

Aside from the obvious differences in method, Clarkson's study differed from the author's in several basic respects. The first difference is favorable to Clarkson; he attempted to predict an actual working decision rather than a surrogate.

The other differences, however, are unfavorable to Clarkson. His method required several orders of magnitude more time to implement than do choice-set representation methods. He was

thus forced to limit himself to a single subject. Even more seriously, he did not specify the steps he took from protocol to constructed decision situations, used in obtaining further protocols, or
even from final protocol to discrimination net model. Thus, his
work remains a tour de force in the realm of art, rather than
measurement. The important point here is that it is very difficult
to generalize his work.

Finally, his validation procedure contains a potentially serious
error. The eighty stocks on the input list for the validation test are
not segregated from those under consideration by the subject during the original protocol recording period. Thus, Clarkson opens
himself to the same well-founded suspicion that I noted concerning this study in Chapter 7. That is, it is not clear to what extent
"accidental" attribute associations present in the original protocol
have been carried along to reproduce the original preference ordering of the same stocks. That is, there may be a problem of autocorrelation of the error term between estimation and validation.
To resolve this, the model should have been tested on a base list of
all-new stocks.

### In Summary

There seem to be two major characteristics for alternative methods
of decision measurement, *feasibility* of measurement operation
and *usefulness* of that operation's result. The most preferred method, of course, depends on the application. It appears that in
applications where feasibility is not very constraining, Clarkson's
method of direct modeling of decision nets dominates the alternatives. However, if feasibility is important then a choice-set method would be more appropriate. Of these, multidimensional scaling,
however, has not been demonstrated to be very feasible when

based on individual attribute data or very useful when based on aggregate, or group, attribute data. Slovic's method of naïve analysis of variance should be used only when the relevant attributes are well known ahead of time. When working with individual decision-makers whose relevant attributes are both little known and variant among different individuals, the method of this book seems generally most appropriate.

# III

Applications

# 9

Applications for the Individual
Decision-Maker

## 9.1. Introduction to Management Applications

The prototype decision-maker for this study is the organizational manager. Of course, in a sense, every decision-maker is a manager of his own affairs. It was suggested in Chapter 1 that advances in managerial planning and control are importantly dependent on increased explicitness. Explicitness refers here to the recording of decision assumptions so that they are distinct and understandable, both to the manager himself and to others in the organization. In the previous chapters, a method of achieving additional explicitness through the measurement of decision assumptions was empirically demonstrated. Examples of the results in a study of stock market participants are shown in Appendixes C and D. In Chapters 9 and 10, some immediate applications of that work are illustrated. In my view, these applications represent powerful tools for improving managerial planning and control processes. These tools derive their usefulness from the measuring procedure developed in Chapter 4. This procedure condenses into separable and explicit attribute components much of what before had often been unconscious, inextricably intertwined, and difficult to analyze.

Before delving into the concrete detail of the suggested application tools, a brief view of current problems in designing and using management information systems for planning and control is in order. In Chapter 1, some limitations of the traditional standard cost accounting systems were noted. In addition, there often arises in practice another important set of problems connected with improper management information system design. Ackoff, an astute commentator on the practice of management, has noted the following.

First, the manager is overwhelmed by data regarding variables irrelevant to his actual decisions. Second, it is difficult to find out what information to supply, partly because the manager himself doesn't know what information he really uses. Third, the manager often needs education on how to use the information provided. Finally, the manager does not use information because he does not understand how it was derived.[1]

Such management information system problems clearly center on a lack of ability by the system designer to gain a sufficient appreciation of the assumptions underlying the manager's decision. However, little work has been done toward providing the designer with a tool for attacking these problems. Existing designers of information systems appear suited neither by training nor temperament for the formal modeling techniques which have been available. On the other hand, naïve questioning of the manager is often inadequate. This follows because decision-makers find it difficult to describe their own assumptions accurately in response to direct, informal questioning. One basic difficulty is that the dimensions used by the decision-maker to characterize the decision situation may be different than those of the questioner. A second problem is that the decision-maker himself may not be consciously aware of the strength of influence of each different attribute on his decision.

A practical formal measurement of decision assumptions may overcome these problems. In such an approach, one elicits from the decision-maker attributes he uses to characterize decision alternatives. Second, one relates statistically the positions of the alternatives along these various attributes to the decision-maker's preferences.

1. See Russell L. Ackoff (1967), for a nice description of "Management Misinformation Systems."

The method of this book attacks both steps in this procedure. It thereby provides a basis for management information system design which is manager-oriented. I contemplate a design process in which the designer would seek to measure the manager's assumptions relevant to his key decisions. He would thus determine what information is likely to be perceived by the manager as relevant, and so would be able to outline an information system that matches the manager's current *perceived* needs. At this step, the problems of discovering relevant data and discarding irrelevant data may be attacked with some expectation of reasonable success. Many management information system designers will undoubtedly find the contemplated design process controversial. They wish to educate the manager, not just freeze him into his existing patterns. However, in my view, an initial dependence on the manager's own perceptions is a sound approach to subsequent attempts to change his behavior through education.

Suppose this first phase of supplying information that the manager already perceives as relevant is complete. Then new kinds of information which the designer feels should be helpful can be supplied to the manager, while his assumptions are monitored. In the process, it is comparatively easy to discover and cure the manager's uncertainty as to how the new data are derived. In addition, explicit measures of individual assumptions that underlie key decisions can be used for comparison with real-world outcomes to help *both* the manager and the systems designer learn how to better use the information provided by the system. This is an appropriate context in which reeducation of the expert manager may take place. In both phases, explicit assumption measurement offers potential for real progress. This chapter offers some provocative illustrations of such applications.

A remaining question for the information system designer is the cost and feasibility of his use of the modeling procedure. The algorithmlike procedure discussed in Chapter 6 does not require a high level of skill to operate. Indeed, it could feasibly be completely computerized. The initial interview and its analysis described in Chapter 5 require somewhat more skill, but of an order which a short period of practice could establish. The time required for the initial interview might average about 1½ hours. To fill out a set of questionnaires containing raw attributes and summary judgments would, at the level of detail encountered here, require an average of 1 to 2 hours.[2] However, in most applications the measurement of assumptions would probably not need to be done more than once or twice per year.

The typical process of organizational management is also to a high degree a multiperson process. In this process *communication* and *combining of judgments*, usually between staff and line or between subordinate and superior, play a very important part. These processes are key aspects of activities through which the organization can behave with better intelligence and judgment than could an individual decision-maker. Chapter 10 provides illustrations of how these processes, too, might be aided by explicit assumption measurement.

Finally, the point should be noted that these results are important not because the measurement procedure developed in this book is the last word. Rather, these results are important because the problems dealt with are so fundamental that even modest progress offers great opportunity for useful application.

2. With interactive computer terminals, everything but the initial interview might be computerized, and even that is open to question. Subsequent assumption measurements might be done cheaply and quickly.

In the remainder of this chapter, applications that a single decision-maker could use with limited resources and without undue disturbance of his organizational context are described. The first of these is simple revision of assumptions on the basis of decision outcome evidence. Second, indications are given for improving the match between the flow of information given to or scanned by the decision-maker and that which actually influences his decision. Third, an illustration for observing changes in his assumptions through time is given, with potential applications for both improved consistency and improved ability to sense changes in supporting information. The application illustrations are based on data taken from my research on the assumptions of participants in the stock market regarding suitability of particular common stocks for the attainment of investment objectives.

## 9.2. Simple Revision of Assumptions Based on Decision Outcome Feedback

Most decision-makers, when first confronted with a new type of decision, seem to learn quickly many of the important factors that bear on the decision's success. Their resulting assumptions are imperfect but useful. After relatively few repetitions, however, these decision-makers usually reach a capability plateau. They may remain capable of partially adapting their assumptions if the environment changes sharply. However, cumulative, self-initiated experimentation and learning, barring such sharp changes, often come to a standstill. For example, in my study of participants in the stock market, many of the experienced trust officers and investors gave all the appearances of using a stable, if inexplicit, decision framework. Yet, most of them appeared fully aware that there was potential for improvement.

Why might this be so? Clearly, one of the basic components of managerial capability is the capacity for self-observation and learning with respect to one's assumptions. Improvements in planning are especially dependent on one's ability to learn from one's mistakes and successes. However, the required self-observation is neither easy nor pleasant. It is obvious that not knowing how to be explicit makes specific assumption inadequacies hard to locate. Beyond this, though, there are emotional difficulties. Everyone experiences psychological discomfort in observing self-inadequacies. In most cases, this leads to inability to continue objective observation. Our view of reality is an integral part of our identity. Thus, we also unconsciously use perceptual defenses against noticing aspects of events which threaten our established view of reality. Of course, these perceptual defenses are not necessarily dysfunctional. They serve to protect us from upsetting existing valid knowledge because of what may be essentially random noise.

The emotional difficulties in self-observation of decision assumptions may be somewhat alleviated through the method of this book. Because of the increased explicitness thereby provided, dissonance between one's assumptions and the evidence of real-world outcomes can be localized. This localization can reduce the psychological threat and pain implicit in a challenge to the decision-maker's overall conceptual framework. Explicit statistical hypothesis testing can be substituted for unconscious perceptual defenses in the legitimate function of rejecting the spurious evidence of statistical noise.

Let us summarize these emotional factors along with "objective" obstacles in the face of revision of decision assumptions. First, when decision outcomes are removed in time from the decision point, learning is made difficult by memory limitations, particularly regarding rejected alternatives. Second, decision-makers notice and remember "evidence" presented by a single crisis much better than numerous small indications of partial assumption failure which are difficult to distinguish from statistical noise. Third, self-observation of one's own assumptions in making a decision is ordinarily imprecise and difficult. Fourth, global, indefinite challenges to one's established viewpoint are more liable to be rejected than localized, specific ones.

For these reasons, a practical, explicit recording of assumptions and a test of them individually against the evidence of decision outcomes is highly desirable. The result will improve the decision-maker's ability to sustain the learning process beyond the mentally comfortable plateau at which, unaided, he would tend to remain.

In order to illustrate how the measurement of decision assumptions might be used for self-observation and learning, three participants from the stock market study were selected. These decision-makers had indicated their investment objectives could be appropriately represented by the price appreciation of the stocks in their portfolios over periods as short as a few months. Thus, their decision assumptions, as measured by Questionnaires 2 and 3, could be well matched against actual market performance over the next few months. The subjects and the dates relevant for the experiment are given in Table 9.1. Factor scores derived from the participant's ratings of nineteen stocks along various attribute scales were calculated.[3]

The participants' direct ratings of the stocks on suitability for

3. There were twenty stocks used in the larger study. One of the stocks was not traded on the exchange throughout the period needed in analyzing these data.

Table 9.1.
Decision Outcome Experiment

| Decision-maker Participant | Type | Assumption Measurement Date | Outcome Checking Date |
|---|---|---|---|
| 07 | professional trader | Sept. 5, 1969 | December 1, 1969 |
| 22 | individual investor | July 29, 1969 | December 1, 1969 |
| 38 | large fund portfolio manager | August 4, 1969 | December 1, 1969 |

investment scales and on various other attribute scales were measured based on Questionnaires 2 and 3 taken at the "assumption date" in Table 9.1. Actual performance of the nineteen stocks was measured in terms of the natural logarithm of the ratio of the stock price at the "outcome checking date" to that of the assumption date.[4] Parenthetically, Appendixes C and D present the pertinent factor structures and assumption measures for these decision-makers. The stocks utilized were given in Table 6.1. The reader might enjoy reviewing these before going on.

Actual stock price performance data $Y^*$ were correlated with each participant's summary perference rating $Y$ for each stock and also regressed against underlying-attribute factor measures $F_k$. Remember that the $Y$ and $F_k$ had previously been related to obtain the assumption measures. For each decision-maker, coincidentally, there were four attribute factors previously tested as significant.

For each of these decision-makers these significant factor scores were forced into a separate stepwise regression. For the purpose of this research, the order of entry was prespecified. Factors with the largest eigenvalues were entered into the regression equation first.

4. The data were adjusted for stock splits but not for dividends.

Table 9.2.
Naïve Decision Outcome Feedback

| Decision-maker | Regression |
|---|---|
| 07 | $Y_{07}^* = 0.02765 + (-0.00054)F_{07\text{-}2}$ <br> $\qquad\qquad\qquad [0.00044]$ <br> $R^2 = .0797$, $F_{1,17} = 1.473$, not significant. |
| 22 | $Y_{22}^* = 0.52210 + (-0.00089)F_{22\text{-}2} + (-0.00061)F_{22\text{-}3}$ <br> $\qquad\qquad\qquad [0.00029] \qquad\qquad [0.00022]$ <br> $R^2 = .4384$, $F_{2,16} = 6.246$, significant at .025 level. |
| 38 | $Y^* = -0.14166 + (-0.00023)\ F_{38\text{-}1} + (-0.00079)F_{38\text{-}2}$ <br> $\qquad\qquad\qquad [0.00064] \qquad\qquad\ [0.00029]$ <br> $R^2 = .3190$, $F_{2,16} = 3.748$, significant at .05 level. |

Note: The significance level figures are based on the usual normality assumptions.

The equations shown in Table 9.2 are the best linear regressions obtained. The coefficients will be more meaningful if reference is made to Table 9.3, where sample means and standard deviations of the $Y$ codes and transformed attribute codes $F_k$ are given. In Table 9.2, standard errors are given in brackets below the coefficients. Thus, there is some evidence that information was available through the attribute factors of Decision-makers 22 and 38 which might potentially be useful. Also, if we look at the simple correlations of preferences $Y$ with actual performance $Y^*$ in Table 9.4, we find the coefficient for the large fund portfolio manager to be fairly large.[5]

The regressions in Table 9.2 would be sufficient in many, perhaps most, problem situations. They suggest useful evidence for

5. It would have appeared more significant if it had not been tested simultaneously with those of two other decision-makers.

Table 9.3.
Means and Standard Deviations of the Codes Used in the Decision Feedback
Experiment

| Variable | Mean | Standard Deviation |
|---|---|---|
| $Y_{07}$ | 469.5 | 284.9 |
| $F_{07-1}$ | 320.0 | 92.0 |
| $F_{07-2}$ | 15.3 | 65.5 |
| $F_{07-4}$ | −479.9 | 79.6 |
| $F_{07-5}$ | 671.7 | 242.4 |
| $Y_{22}$ | 457.9 | 325.4 |
| $F_{22-1}$ | −205.3 | 139.2 |
| $F_{22-2}$ | 68.0 | 114.0 |
| $F_{22-3}$ | 639.5 | 155.5 |
| $F_{22-6}$ | − 34.6 | 67.7 |
| $Y_{38}$ | 473.7 | 303.8 |
| $F_{38-1}$ | − 94.3 | 46.5 |
| $F_{38-2}$ | −168.7 | 101.3 |
| $F_{38-4}$ | 351.5 | 51.3 |
| $F_{38-5}$ | − 83.3 | 126.7 |

Table 9.4.
Correlations of Preferences and Later Real-World Performance, Uncorrected
for the Market Factor

| | |
|---|---|
| corr. $(Y_{07}^{*}, Y_{07}) = .278$ | $R^2 = .077$ |
| corr. $(Y_{22}^{*}, Y_{22}) = .071$ | $R^2 = .005$ |
| corr. $(Y_{38}^{*}, Y_{38}) = .462$ | $R^2 = .213$ |

adjusting the decision assumptions measured toward those shown to be predictive of actual real-world outcomes.

Unfortunately for purposes of simple illustration, in the case of the stock market these results are deceptive. The statistical tests of significance assume independence of observations. In fact, we know that returns to individual stocks are highly intercorrelated with the performance of the market as a whole. About all we can say from these statistics is that there are indications that $Y_{38}$, $F_{22-2}$, $F_{22-3}$, and $F_{38-2}$ have either face validity as predictors of differential stock performance *or else* that they appear predictors of differential performance *given* a valid prediction of the direction of the market as a whole. Since the attribute of "stock volatility" would satisfy the latter requirement, and since this attribute is already well known, the foregoing results are not yet very useful.

However, if we partial out the variance associated with that of the market as a whole, we can base the regression on what are much more nearly independent observations. To do this, the closing prices on the first trading day of each month from January 1967 through June 1969 were recorded for each of the nineteen stocks and for the Dow-Jones Industrial Average. For each stock the natural logarithm of month-to-month price ratios, adjusted for stock-splits (though not for dividends) was regressed as a simple linear function of the same series for the Dow-Jones Industrial Average. The equation thus obtained for each stock gave a measure of the expected variance in stock performance explainable by the action of the market as a whole.[6] This equation was used to partial out from the actual outcome data the variance to

6. This regression coefficient is a measure of the now famous "$\beta$" of modern portfolio theory; see Sharpe (1964) and Jensen (1970).

be expected from market movement on the basis of this linear model. The residuals that remain are the actual outcome data unexplained by the market factor. Systematic intercorrelation due to industry factors appears negligible in this set of observations, but could also have been partialled out as a further refinement.

Let us label these residual outcomes $Y'$. Following the same prespecified stepwise regression procedure as before, the best estimates shown in Table 9.5 were obtained. They are similar to, but slightly weaker than, those obtained before adjusting for the market factor.

Thus, there is *some* evidence that each of the decision-makers, particularly Decision-maker 22, had access to information potentially useful in predicting stock performance not dependent in a linear fashion on a prediction of the market as a whole.[7] This information is contained in the attribute factor measures $F_k$.

In our illustration, the next question is whether the decision-makers actually use the valid attribute information in the $F_k$ when making their ratings. If we look at the correlations of the preference ratings $Y$ with the residual performances $Y'$, we obtain the data of Table 9.6.

What lessons can now be drawn? It appears plausible that Subjects 07 and 38 are using valid information. In the case of Subject 07, the valid information may be greater than that potentially available through the measured attribute factors $F_k$. It is, however, quite likely that Subject 22 is *misusing* any information poten-

7. This evidence should not be overvalued, since it might possibly be accounted for by a number of other factors, such as the exclusion of dividends or nonnormality. I am, of course, aware that this finding is superficially counter to the trend of the last ten years of research in the field of finance. That research has failed to uncover any substantial ability by market participants to predict stock performance. See my comments in Section 12.2.

Table 9.5
Corrected Decision Outcome Feedback

| Decision-maker | Regression |
|---|---|
| 07 | $Y'_{07} = 0.03306 + (-0.00065)F_{07\text{-}2}$ <br> $\qquad\qquad [0.00045]$ <br> $R^2 = .1101, F_{1,17} = 2.103$, significant at the 0.20 level. |
| 22 | $Y'_{22} = 0.45633 + (-0.00086)F_{22\text{-}2} + (-0.00053)F_{22\text{-}3}$ <br> $\qquad\qquad [0.00029] \qquad\qquad [0.00021]$ <br> $R^2 = .4097, F_{2,16} = 5.553$, significant at the 0.05 level. |
| 38 | $Y'_{38} = -0.13002 + (-0.00023)F_{38\text{-}1} + (-0.00076)F_{38\text{-}2}$ <br> $\qquad\qquad [0.00066] \qquad\qquad [0.00030]$ <br> $R^2 = .2890, F_{2,16} = 3.251$, significant at the 0.10 level. |

Table 9.6.
Correlations of Preference Ratings with Residual Performances

| | |
|---|---|
| corr. $(Y'_{07}, Y_{07}) = 0.408,$ | $R^2 = .1665$ <br> significant at 0.10 level |
| corr. $(Y'_{22}, Y_{22}) = 0.040,$ | $R^2 = .0016$ <br> not significant |
| corr. $(Y'_{38}, Y_{38}) = 0.441$ | $R^2 = .1945$ <br> significant at 0.10 level |

tially available to him through the $F_k$. In the work described in Chapter 6, the following was obtained as a measure of his assumptions:

$$Y_{22} = 2873 + (-1.94)F_{22\text{-}1} + (-2.93)F_{22\text{-}3} + (-1.54)F_{22\text{-}6}.$$

Thus, he placed reliance not only on $F_{22\text{-}3}$, which our evidence indicates was helpful, but also on $F_{22\text{-}1}$ and $F_{22\text{-}6}$, which were not, and ignored $F_{22\text{-}2}$, which our evidence indicates would have been quite useful. There is even a little evidence that he placed the wrong sign on $F_{22\text{-}1}$, since regression of actual outcome data gave

$$Y'_{22} = 0.30883 + (0.00057)F_{22\text{-}1} + (-0.00085)F_{22\text{-}2}$$
$$[0.00034]$$
$$+ (0.00012)F_{22\text{-}3}.$$

As a sidelight, Subject 22 in his original interview had contrasted what he felt to be his past dependence on "fundamental" analysis with his present reliance on "technical" or "chartist" analysis. This change would apparently correspond to a shift from $F_{22\text{-}2}$ to reliance on $F_{22\text{-}3}$. In the practical use of the presently proposed application of measured assumptions, the evidence presented should act as a signal to him that he ought to consider the greater use of his presently underused "fundamental" analysis.

Use of Analysis

This kind of feedback evidence or learning information can, of course, be beneficially used by the decision-maker to revise or confirm his *implicit* assumptions. However, it could also be used to revise an *explicit* model of his assumptions, such as those which were estimated in Chapter 6.

Thus, for example, the models earlier obtained by the assumption measurement were the following:

$$Y_{07} = 523.0 + (-3.110)F_{7\text{-}2},$$
$$Y_{22} = 2872.8 + (-1.941)F_{22\text{-}1} + (-2.926)F_{22\text{-}3}$$
$$+ (-1.542)F_{22\text{-}6},$$
$$Y_{38} = 347.7 + (0.989)F_{38\text{-}1} + (-1.292)F_{38\text{-}2}.$$

Such models could be maintained by the decision-maker as a kind of backup check device against which his actual utilization of his existing subjective knowledge could be compared. The learning information gained through the preceding evidence could be applied to these models to change the coefficients by which each attribute factor is weighted to arrive at a decision. In this manner, the already-estimated models of the manager's existing assumptions could be updated on the basis of the new evidence. Various strategies for incorporating learning information into the models could be used. One of the simplest would be to estimate the "best" predictor equation with actual consequence data, here the actual percentage price changes. Then, one could make incremental adjustments of the prior existing model toward the newly estimated "best" predictor equation with each new set of actual consequence data.

That is, let

$$Y_t = b_0 + b_1 F_1 + b_2 F_2 + \ldots + b_m F_m$$

be the existing assumption at time $t$. Let

$$Y' = b_0' + b_1' F_1 + b_2' F_2 + \ldots + b_m' F_m$$

be the "best" model from the new data set or learning situation Then let

$$Y_{t+1} = Y_t + \frac{b_0' - b_0'}{\gamma_0} + \frac{b_1' - b_1}{\gamma_1} F_1 + \ldots + \frac{b_m' - b_m}{\gamma_m} F_m .$$

where $\gamma_k$, $k = 1, \ldots, m$ are parameters greater than unity which govern the sensitivity of the model to new learning information along various $F_k$.

The foregoing learning procedure is not suggested as optimal in a maximum likelihood sense; indeed, it has some drawbacks. It is merely suggested as a simple example of what might fruitfully be used by practical decision-makers.

## 9.3. Measured Assumptions as a Guide to Information Search

Suppose a decision-maker is confronted with a choice regarding alternatives about which he knows little. Ordinarily, he will search for more information regarding the alternatives before making his choice. A widespread and interesting class of problems arises from the need to predict the kinds of information for which he will look. An important member of this class is the problem of designing effective information systems to support managerial decision-making.[8]

The reader may readily extrapolate the example from the stock market in this section to other examples from his own experience.

The pertinent information for current choices is generally data relating to the attributes that figure most strongly in the attribute factors assumed by the decision-maker to be important.

Suppose the decision-maker is not aware in detail of the information of which he makes use in coming to a decision. This uncertainty is often the case in reality. Models of assumptions, such as those given in Appendix D, can provide an insight into the decision-maker's probable information use. For example, in the case of Subject 38, we have the model

$$Y_{38} = 347.7 + (0.989)F_{38\text{-}1} + (-1.292)F_{38\text{-}2}.$$

It should be noted that the complexity of this model could very well be greater if it were based on a larger sample of observations. The factor measures $F_{38\text{-}1}$ and $F_{38\text{-}2}$ are based on the factor structure shown in Table 9.7. The poles at the left represent a high score for the factor, those at the right a low score. The numbers in the left-hand column in the figure are factor loadings. They repre-

8. Some others include curriculum design in education, advertising, and counter-intelligence maneuvers. See Section 10.3.

Table 9.7.
Factor Structure of Assumed Relevant Attributes — Subject 38

**Factor I ($F_{38\text{-}1}$ )**

| | |
|---|---|
| .88 stock has appreciated a great deal recently | stock has declined a great deal recently |
| .97 is a very fashionable stock at present | presently in market disfavor |
| .88 not so | viewed as a conglomerate |
| .95 made new highs for the year very recently | closer to its lows than its highs for the year |

**Factor II ($F_{38\text{-}2}$ )**

| | |
|---|---|
| .91 so vast it's beyond comprehension, predictable | not so |
| .91 stock price based on dividends | not so |
| .76 company less aggressively managing its assets than in the past | company more aggressively managing its assets than in the past |
| .74 old style, sleepy | not so |

sent the correlation of the factor with the codes for the raw attribute listed.

Based on the evidence obtained through regressions with residual stock price performance as presented in Section 9.2, $F_{38\text{-}2}$ has only weak evidence of being useful, and $F_{38\text{-}1}$ is apparently no help at all. However, as an alternative to assumption revision, Subject 38 might investigate the adequacy of the information on an individual stock's position along various attribute scales which he is given by his staff or through his own search.

It has been suggested by my research that there are major differences between decision-makers. These differences lie not only in their assumptions about particular stocks but also in their assumptions as to which attributes should be used to characterize stocks in order to select among stocks. Our analysis has been focused entirely on the second type of assumption — on which *attributes*

of stocks are means to an investment end. However, once these
latter are measured, it becomes more fruitful to examine the first
type. We can then ask more fruitfully to what degree a particular
stock does possess some attribute.

In this context, we may examine attributes underlying Subject
38's $F_{38-1}$ and $F_{38-2}$, on which he appears to rely. How good is
the decision-maker's state of information regarding the position of
the various stocks along those factors. For example, $F_{38-1}$ is
loaded heavily on

"is a very fashionable stock                    "presently in market
at present"                                      disfavor".

Knowing the importance of this factor and this contributory raw
attribute in his decision, Decision-maker 38 is now in a better
position to seek additional raw attribute measures that can contribute to this factor, or to seek improved accuracy along the existing raw data attributes that have heavy loadings, such as the one
shown earlier. Thus, as a result of our analysis, he might well
make, for example, a greater effort to collect improved information relevant to deciding whether a stock was "fashionable" or
not. In general, this would be an appropriate context in which to
decide what information should be furnished to him by organizational information systems such as the accounting system or, in
this case, by the security analyst. As a further heuristic, since there
is a little evidence $F_{38-2}$ has greater real predictive value, more
emphasis might be placed on data relevant to it rather than on $F_{38-1}$.
In particular, use of security analysts or personal visits might be
directed toward paying particular attention to $F_{38-2}$ attributes, like
changes in "management's aggressiveness in managing its assets,"
in order to further exploit the apparent predictive value of $F_{38-2}$.

The points made in the foregoing paragraph obviously apply

also to attributes associated with any presently unused factors indicated by statistical evidence as potentially predictive of real-world decision outcomes.

**This Application Broadly Considered**

The use of measured assumptions to guide information search can be made in a variety of fields. One can thereby examine the relevance of existing organizational, staff, and individualized information support. Whenever it is being determined that information provided does not match the decision-maker's types of relevant and usable attributes for characterizing decision alternatives, there are two choices. These are to improve the information supply or to improve the decision assumptions. Both choices, improving intelligence information and educating the decision-maker, critically depend on effective identification of the used and unused information.[9] The application of the measurement of assumptions noted in the foregoing appears to represent marked progress here.

**9.4. Observation of Consistency and Systematic Changes in Measured Assumptions**

The assumption measure application that appears to come most readily to the minds of practicing managers is that of checking them for consistency.[10] Perhaps the reader may be persuaded that

---

9. This gives a hint as to the possibility of the use of measured assumptions generally in making education in new concepts more effective. See also Chapter 11.

10. Some operations researchers have gathered evidence that consistent decisions provide superior average performance; see Bowman (1963). One could investigate the available data used in this study to determine whether as predictors of actual stock performances the predicted preference ratings were superior to the actual preference ratings. That is, one could investigate whether the inconsistencies not captured in the model were predictive of actual stock performance.

such prosaic checks for consistency may also be put to other uses than mere enforcement of current rationality.

The urge for consistency stems from an implicit acceptance of the normative microeconomic current performance model of decision-making discussed in Chapter 3. Within reasonable cognitive limitations this is a valid norm. However, this microeconomic framework presumes an existing set of assumptions linking an existing class of attributes to preferences. It implies a normative behavior given this presumption. It has no implication whatever for the other real-world problem for the individual decision-maker of discovering new attributes relevant to his preferences!

It is clear that the addition of some experimental or even random components to one's decision-making responses to problems is an extremely useful contributor to the discovery of new relevant attributes.[11] Thus, there is an implication that learning of new concepts may be impeded by too much consistency.[12]

On the other hand, clearly both current performance and efficient learning can be impeded by too little consistency. Thus, a long-run virtue of repeated assumption measures might well be a greater understanding of an appropriate range of consistency for various problem domains.

In the stock market example of this section, some notions of how one can use repeated assumption measures as signals for learning are offered.

One can apply measures of assumptions repeated over time not only to promote current assumption rationality and learning, but

11. See Wiener (1948). Bowman explicitly recognized this phenomenon in the article cited in the previous footnote.
12. Here, *concept* is used as an attribute or combination of attributes employed in a decision net.

also to explicitly signal unconscious perceptions of changes in the source of attribute information and in the problem environment.

At this level, the potential use for such repeated measures lies in monitoring —

1. consistency for both current performance and learning,
2. learning trends,
3. unconscious responses to shifts in information availability, in the problem environment, or in the characteristics of the alternatives.

At a lower level, one may also monitor the typically more frequent fluctuations in the perception of the position of a decision alternative along the relevant attributes.

## Stock Market Example

Decision-maker 22 is used as a simple example of the application of assumption measures to observing changes. We can analyze some basic aspects of his changes over time simply by constructing the correlations of his attribute factor measures and summary preference ratings at two points in time, and subtracting one from the other. In the stock market study described in Chapters 4 through 7, data were gathered regarding assumptions and then tested against new data collected several months later. Subtracting the first correlations of the factor scores ($F_k$) and the preference rating ($Y$) from the same correlations derived from the second data set, we obtain the results shown in Table 9.8.

The statistical significance of such shifts is a very complicated function of the true population correlation matrix.[13] However, at the place of maximum expected sample variance, where the population simple correlations are zero, the complicated distribution

13. See Anderson (1958).

Table 9.8.
Shifts in Correlations over Time — Subject 22

|            | First $R_{YF_k}$ | Second $R_{YF_k}$ | Shift |
|------------|------------------|-------------------|-------|
| $F_{22\text{-}1}$ | .10   | −.26 | −.36 |
| $F_{22\text{-}2}$ | −.18  | −.88 | −.70 |
| $F_{22\text{-}3}$ | −.48  | .05  | .53  |
| $F_{22\text{-}6}$ | .28   | .21  | −.07 |

simplifies. In this case, for sample size $N$ and for simple pairwise correlations $R$, the statistic

$$\frac{R^2/1}{(1 - R^2)/(N - 2)}$$

is distributed as Fisher's $F_{1,N-2}$ for a normal multivariate population. For Subject 22, a shift in $R$ greater than .43 is significant at the 5 percent level. If the population $R$ is not equal to zero, shifts of this magnitude would be more significant.

In this case, the evidence indicates a strong increase in reliance on $F_{22\text{-}2}$ and a decrease in reliance on $F_{22\text{-}3}$ in coming to the preference $Y_{22}$. The meaning of such strong shifts will usually be explicable to the decision-maker. For example, Subject 22 later informed the author, without knowing of these results, that a temporary lack of currency in the "technical" stock information available to him for the second data set might have invalidated these data with respect to the model resulting from the first data set. The foregoing report of shifts clearly indicates this important event, as can be seen in the positive poles of $F_{22\text{-}2}$ and $F_{22\text{-}3}$ shown in Table 9.9.

This kind of data on shifting assumptions would be of somewhat greater usefulness if several, rather than just two, measuring

Table 9.9
Positive Poles of Factors Whose Usage Had Shifted — Subject 22

| Factor II (22-2) |
| --- |
| .83 demand for final use products indicates lack of growth |
| .88 serves consumer market |
| .82 decline in earnings |
| .77 fortunes tied to factors beyond company's control |
| .75 past performance has been worse than expected |
| .71 in highly competitive business where they are non-unique |

Factor III (22-3)
.85 short-term technical demand is weak
.76 long-term technical demand is worsening
.76 short-term technical demand is worsening
.82 stock price has recently moved down by a large percentage

points in time had been taken; in that case, one could more easily distinguish "steady-state" decision-maker inconsistency over time from other kinds of operationally significant changes in assumptions.

The usefulness of this kind of signal as to probable changes in information flow could be expected to be greatest when the decision process was informal and inexplicit.

## Monitoring Changes in Assumptions as a Guide to New Explicit Concepts

In the validation test of Chapter 7, the assumption measure of Subject 3 was invalidated for a superficially incongruous reason. The $R^2$ between his actual preferences and the preferences predicted by his measured assumptions was significantly different from zero. However, the model was invalidated since $R < 0$. This signals a possible shift in assumptions by the subject in response to environmental changes. It points to a phenomenon present in a number of subjects' decision processes, and is particularly clear in this case.

The evidence supports the validity of the model's focus on the attribute factor in question as *relevant* to the decision-maker's preferences. However, there appears to be an inconsistency in the way the attribute is used. In the first instance, it apparently caused the decision-maker to prefer conservative stocks. In the second instance, it led to preference for risky or aggressive stocks. The explanation of course, is that in the first case the market as a whole had just gone through a long decline. In the second case, the market as a whole had been rising. Apparently, Subject 3 was extrapolating the movement of the market. If he thought the market was going up, he correctly assumed aggressive stocks were a better buy, and vice versa. Thus, we are led as outside observers to a new attribute, which might conceivably be labeled

"degree of volatility well suited for the forecasted market environment"

"degree of volatility not well suited for the forecasted market environment".

To see how a decision-maker could be himself led to initially discover such relevant new attributes, consider a new situation. In this case, it is not the equation for decision assumptions which exhibits significant coefficient sign reversal over time. Rather, the equation relating real-world stock performance to factor attributes exhibits statistically significant fluctuation in coefficients. The decision-maker thus receives a signal that should excite his interest to explore in order to discover an associated attribute of the stock, or of some other aspect of the problem environment.

Once this associate is identified, the decision-maker constructs a conjunction of the original attribute that exhibited fluctuating coefficients and the associated attribute newly discovered. This conjunction defines a novel attribute that may be relabeled and that should serve as a guide to future preferences in similar decision situations. Such discovery of novel attributes is fundamental to creative theory building in general.

Parenthetically, one aspect of this process is the continual recasting of attributes exhibiting nonlinear interaction effects on preferences in terms of new attributes that do not exhibit such interaction effects. This may be a major reason why linear measures of decision assumptions are as effective as they are.

### In Summary

To begin this chapter, we noted some overriding problems in the design of management information systems. On a smaller scale, they are applicable to anyone who makes moderately repetitive decisions relying on information furnished by others. First, the manager is overwhelmed by data regarding variables irrelevant to his actual decisions. Second, it is difficult to find out what information to supply, partly because the manager himself doesn't know what information he really uses. Third, the manager and the system designer often need education on the best use of the information provided. Finally, the manager does not use information because he doesn't understand it, but no corrective feedback to the information system designer is provided. These problems center on a lack of ability by the information system designer to gain a sufficient appreciation of the manager's decision assumptions and their individual merits. This lack may be considerably relieved through the use of the methods described in this book.

Several examples from the stock market participant study have been given to illustrate methods for such applications. These examples pay special attention to three specific applications: increasing decision-maker learning from experience, improving information supply, and monitoring decision assumption consistency. They are all available to the individual decision-maker who has limited resources.

# 10

Applications for Multiperson
Decision Contexts

One may define two broad classes of applications for measures of
decision assumptions in a multiperson context. In the first class,
one supposes continuing cooperation. Applications in aggregate
decision-making and communication are of this type. In the second class, one does not assume continuing cooperation. Applications such as marketing research fall into this category.

To indicate the main features of the measurement method of
this book in these areas, the three sections of this chapter examine
its application to aggregate decisions, communication, and marketing research.

It should be particularly noted that in this chapter "preference
rating" is used to mean "decision."[1]

## 10.1. Improving Aggregate Decision-making through Better Combination of Assumptions

Different people very often make different decisions in objectively
similar situations because they use different attributes to characterize the situation and because they weight these attributes
differently in coming to their decisions. These differences can
sometimes be exploited to produce an aggregate decision which, in
some sense, is more intelligent than one that relies only on the
usefulness of the assumptions of a single decision-maker. This
strategy of producing improved "effectiveness" through aggregate
decision-making is a primary characteristic of successful organizations. It is possible, however, for an aggregate decision to be less
intelligent, on the average, than any of its component individual
contributors. Thus, *the method of aggregation of individual as-*

1. We are in this chapter supposing the microeconomic model of decision-
making, leaving out only convexity of preference regions.

*sumptions* is a key determinant of organizational, and societal, success.[2]

At a very elementary level, some scientific work has been done on the usefulness of various forms of aggregation. In an illuminating experiment in the early 1950s on the prediction of actual social and technological events, it was found that prediction success by individuals could be improved upon by putting the individuals into discussion groups. The discussion group predictions, however, were in turn inferior to predictions made by the experimenters' mathematically *averaging* the predictions made by non-interacting individuals. This is one of few instances of serious evidence on this issue known to this investigator.[3] It supports the adage that "two heads are better than one" but offers the interesting thought that two independent judgments may often be even better, if properly aggregated.

The general topic of improving methods of assumption aggregation is fascinating and relatively uncharted. However, one can make clear some basic issues with the following simple example.

Suppose for the $i$th decision-maker asked to make some particular decision alone, there exists a decision variable $Y_i$ based on a linear function of $m_i$ assumptions relating to attribute factors $F_{ij}$, where $j = 1, \ldots, m_i$:

$$Y_i = a_{i0} + a_{i1} F_{i1} + \ldots + a_{ij} F_{ij} + \ldots + a_{im_i} F_{im_i}.$$

2. Probably the most highly developed of such mechanisms extant is the stock market itself. Note, however, that in this sense an aggregate decision does not imply conscious cooperation among the individual decision-makers.
3. See Kaplan, Skogstad, and Girshick (1950). In the last decade, this finding has been supported by studies on the effectiveness of the Delphi method of technological forecasting; see Dalkey (1969).

Thus, for example, in determining the best of a number of decision alternatives, the decision-maker may be represented as rating them along the $F_{ij}$ and then combining these ratings to get a final preference rating $Y_i$.

Of course, this simple model assumes both that the $F_{ij}$ ratings are metric and that there are no interaction terms among the assumptions, which is only roughly the case in the data from the stock market study described in this book. Given this simple model, how should such decision-makers best be aggregated? In Table 10.1, some rather different decision aggregation mechanisms are presented for the case where there are only two decision-makers. They by no means exhaust the possibilities. The aggregate decision preference rating is labeled $Y$. An important and interesting class of aggregation procedures not shown are those derivable from various voting mechanisms.[4]

In Table 10.1, the first type of combination shown, nonhierarchical independent judgment, corresponds to that used for the best predictions in the Kaplan et al. study, with $b_1 = b_2$.

The second type, hierarchical but quasi-independent judgment, is more flexible. If $b_{1j} = c$, a constant for all $j$, it is equivalent to Type 1. Otherwise, the $b_{1j}$ represent a reweighting by Decision-maker 1 of the importance attached to various attributes by Decision-maker 2. In all Type 2 combined judgments, however, the full set of decision alternatives is transmitted to Decision-maker 1.

The third type probably corresponds more closely than the other two to most real-world combined judgments. In this type,

---

4. See Tullock (1967). A well-known theorem by Arrow notes that a complete preference ordering by each of the individuals does not guarantee a complete preference ordering obtained through a simple voting mechanism. Some of these voting mechanisms make choice-set representation infeasible.

Table 10.1.
Three Common Types of Aggregations of Linear Assumptions

| | |
|---|---|
| **Type 1**<br>Nonhierarchical,<br>independent<br>judgment | $Y = b_1 \left( \sum_{j=1}^{m_1} a_{1j} F_{1j} \right) + b_2 \left( \sum_{j=1}^{m_2} a_{2j} F_{2j} \right)$ |
| **Type 2**<br>Hierarchical, but<br>quasi-independent<br>judgment | $Y = b_1 \left( \sum_{j=1}^{m_1} a_{1j} F_{1j} \right) + \sum_{j=1}^{m_2} b_{1j} (a_{2j} F_{2j})$ |
| **Type 3**<br>Hierarchical, sequential<br>interaction judgment | $Y = b_1 \left( \sum_{j=1}^{m_1} a_{1j} F_{1j} \right) + \sum_{j=1}^{m_2} b_{1j} (a_{2j} F_{2j}),$ <br><br>for that subset of alternatives for which <br><br>$\left( \sum_{j=1}^{m_2} a_{2j} F_{2j} \right) \geqslant C_2$ |

only a subset of the alternatives considered by Decision-maker 2 is communicated to Decision-maker 1.[5] This corresponds to the organizational "screening process" often noted. The Type 3 screening process introduces nonlinear interactions between the $F_{1j}$ and the $F_{2j}$ in affecting aggregate preferences.

Decision processes incorporating Type 3 screening of alternatives are thus, in general, more difficult to model through the simple regression approach used in this book. In severe cases, it may be more convenient to retreat to a direct decision-net model than to attempt a choice-set representation.[6]

5. Parenthetically, in such a Type 3 process, the convexity of the preference regions for the individuals does not guarantee the same properties for the aggregation.
6. A choice-set representation is still possible in Type 3 aggregation of linear assumptions if we can somehow assign a meaningful preference rating for the screened-out alternatives. However, the preference regions generally do not possess desirable topological properties. See Section 3.1.

How can explicit measurement of assumptions of individual participants aid in aggregate forecasting or decision-making? Clearly, those aids to the individual decision-maker described in Chapter 9 are also aids in aggregate decision-making. These were assumption revision based on actual outcome data, the guiding of information search, and the monitoring of assumption changes and consistency over time.

What else is available? Consider the following problem. Aggregate decisions in organizations are very often hierarchical in nature, as when staff or middle management provide top management with recommendations on which to base a final decision. One conjectures that most of these decisions are Type 3.

Let us regard Decision-maker 1 as being the superior of Decision-maker 2. Their aggregate decision is expressed as Type 3 in Table 10.1. The reweighting by the superior of his subordinate's assumptions is accomplished through the $b_{1j}$ coefficients. If the superior has little knowledge of the explicit assumptions used by Decision-maker 2, then $b_{1j} = c$, for all $j$. That is, the summary decision recommendations are passed along from the subordinate to the superior, but the explicit assumptions on which the recommendations are based are not available, or are not communicated clearly. Without this knowledge, the superior can not reweight the assumptions of the subordinate (as in Type 2) in arriving at his decisions but must weight the subordinate's decision process taken as a whole. Worse, he can have little confidence that the "screened out" alternatives are undesirable.

This difficulty appears common in management staff-line relationships where the staff is unable to communicate the models used in arriving at recommendations for line management.

Clearly, when our simple linear aggregation model is used, the potential effectiveness of the aggregate decision is usually raised if this restriction is removed. If the superior can individually re-weight each assumption of the subordinate decision-maker, he can potentially arrive at the best possible linear aggregation of assumptions regarding the alternatives transmitted to him.

The following example shows how appropriate $b_{1j}$ weights for best linear assumption aggregation can be derived. We shall use the naïve best models of decision actual outcomes developed first in Section 9.2.[7]

In the stock market study, Subject 22 recorded attribute and preference ratings in Questionnaires 2 and 3 a week before Subject 38. Could Subject 38 have used Subject 22's independent view-point in coming to his own judgment? A partial answer is supplied in Figure 10.1. This figure shows the result of a regression run to estimate the best predictor of the actual stock price performance data relevant for Subject 38. In this estimation, the stepwise regression algorithm was allowed to pick from the 8 previously significant factor measures (4 each for Subjects 22 and 38) the best predictors of actual performance. The answer to the question is that indeed there is a potential for improvement, which might be realized by Subject 38 incorporating the attributes $F_{22-1}$ and $F_{22-2}$ into his judgment.

Thus, as a signal for further exploration, the regression run was valuable. However, this run does not in itself give convincing evidence that the potential is realizable with fresh data; the combination of $F_{22-1}$ and $F_{22-2}$ does not quite meet the modified statistical test based for $k = 8$. The fact that the stepwise package

7. The extra step of removing the market factor from the individual stock performances seemed unnecessary to repeat in order to illustrate the basic method used here.

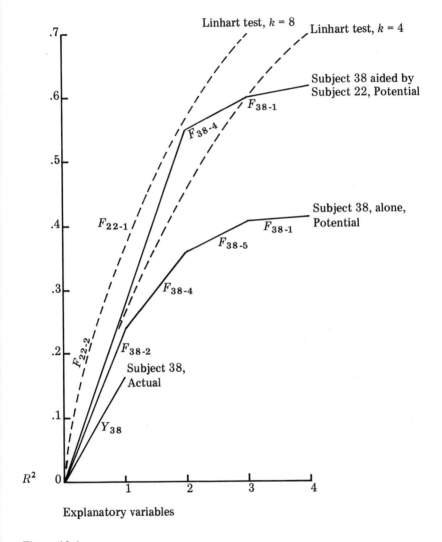

Figure 10.1
Maximum Joint Potential, Subjects 22 and 38

was allowed to select from 8 explanatory variables required that a statistical test of the significance of the additional $R^2$ explanation be made quite strict. If some kind of a priori evidence had indicated that $F_{22-2}$ and $F_{22-1}$ should be forced into the equation alone, the combination would have easily passed the correspondingly less severe test. Of course, here such would be the case in a new trial with the fresh data available from Questionnaires 4 and 5. This is another strong reason for gathering a validating data set after the initial measure of assumptions.

The method just outlined is, in this view, a useful approach to the problem of constructing objective, explicit methods of combining subjective judgments from more than one decision-maker. It requires a somewhat larger sample of observations than required for applications by one individual because more degrees of freedom are exhausted by the larger number of variables. This need was implied in the foregoing when one set of observations was used up in zeroing in on appropriate variables with which to attempt combination.

Once such explicit assumptions and best aggregation parameters have been estimated, it then becomes possible to appraise the future opportunity loss of subordinates' not making explicit their assumptions. Similarly, one might conduct studies to appraise the effect of screening of alternatives by subordinates. Though much empirical work remains to be done to test the feasibility of this application, it seems a promising approach.

### 10.2. Use of Measured Assumptions and Common Referents to Improve Communication

This section contains the germ of a mathematical theory of communication. It makes an admittedly utopian proposal. In my view, however, improvements in communication will ultimately be the most important application of measures of assumptions.

In the previous section, the application of measured assumptions to multiperson coordinative judgments was discussed. An implicit assumption in that discussion for Type 2 and Type 3 combined judgments was that the requisite communication from Decision-maker 2 to Decision-maker 1 could be achieved. In that discussion, such a supposition was reasonable because we were dealing with a stable framework of repetitive decisions and large numbers of alternatives to serve as communication referents.

Such a supposition is *not* justified in most communication contexts. Usually, the recipient of a message must interpret it within the framework of concepts not well adapted to the relevant decision, set of referents, and attribute ordering which the message's sender may have had in mind. Let us look at two examples.

Suppose the message is the sentence, "this movie is long." In order to *understand fully* the message here, it is necessary to have an appreciation for two aspects. First, one must know the set of movies or other objects with which this movie is being compared. Second, one must know how the sender's measure of longness corresponds to the recipient's measure of longness — that is, the mapping from the sender's ordered set of movies to the recipient's ordered set of movies.

On the other hand, suppose the message is the sentence, "this movie is *too* long." Now the recipient must also appreciate the decision and its assumptions which the sender has in mind. For example, a movie could be too long for television without being too long to be shown successfully at a downtown theater.

It is the point of this section to show how the foregoing requirements for good communication can be attacked through the explicit measurement of decision assumptions. Clearly, such applications will be justified only in the case of significant communication problems. However, these seem to be in abundance.

To illustrate the costs of lack of communication, even in a simple case, consider the joint decision-making problem of Section 10.1. Suppose in Type 2 aggregation that Decision-maker 2 could not for some reason communicate his underlying separable attribute factors, even though he could communicate his summary preference rating. Then Decision-maker 1 would be forced to make his judgment based purely on his overall faith in Decision-maker 2. This clearly lowers the potential for optimum usage of the information in the $F_{2j}$'s relevant to the decision.

Thus, one would suspect, even if one did not know it already from personal experience, that explicit communication of assumptions is of great value in multiperson planning and control processes.

### Value-Free, Single-Attribute Communication

Suppose for each communicant some attribute is defined as a partly or completely ordered set. The members of this set are all the referents that he has experienced and classified along that attribute. Now suppose for two communicants there is a one-to-one correspondence between the members of these two sets. The nature of this one-to-one correspondence is known to both individuals.[8] Therefore, perfect communication is possible between these two attributes if the discussed referent is already classified by both participants. If, however, one individual wishes to communicate his classification of a *new* referent, another property may be required for perfect communication. This requirement

8. This correspondence is a bijective mapping. See Bourbaki (1968) for a description of its properties.

is nothing less than that both attributes be completely ordered sets. In addition, perfect communication is feasible in a practical sense only if the functional mapping between sets is rather simple.[9]

The foregoing perfect communication is probably rarely, if ever, realized in practice. Clearly, however, communication efforts can tolerate a good deal of imperfection and still sustain considerable real-world cooperation. Let's review some mechanisms that contribute to more nearly perfect communication.

There are two theoretical ways one can improve simple single-attribute communication. First, one can re-form the attributes so that a simpler, more nearly one-to-one correspondence exists, and thus can potentially be modeled. Second, one can model the existing mapping or correspondence between attributes.

In real-world practice, the activities known as explanation and interpretation usually involve both these components, re-forming attributes and modeling existing correspondences between attributes. The use of shared real-world referents is often indispensable at some stage of modeling the existing mappings. In a less obvious way, shared referents can contribute to re-forming the attributes so that a more nearly one-to-one correspondence exists between them.

Let us illustrate these two steps with respect to Subjects 22 and 38. First, we will suppose the set of referents is given. Suppose

9. In Shannon's information theory both attributes (attribute ordered sets) are assumed identical and in one-to-one correspondence with the real line. His analysis of channel capacity therefore is limited to just one type of communication difficulty, the difficulty of transmitting to the recipient specifications of small subsets of the attribute ordered set of the sender. Semantic communication problems are not dealt with. See Shannon (1949). The theory hinted in this section *is* capable of dealing with such problems.

Subject 38 is trying to "understand" messages sent by Subject 22 along the attribute factor $F_{22-2}$. He can try to interpret $F_{22-2}$ in terms of his own constructs $F_{38-1}$, $F_{38-2}$, $F_{38-4}$, and $F_{38-5}$. Since among the real-world referents of both Subject 22 and Subject 38 are the same set of twenty stocks, observed a little less than a week apart, an approximate linear mapping interpretation can be obtained by the multiple regression model:

$$F_{22-2} = b_0 + b_1 F_{38-1} + b_2 F_{38-2} + b_4 F_{38-4} + b_5 F_{38-5}.$$

When the coefficients of this model are estimated with stepwise regression, the results shown in Figure 10.2 are obtained. The regression is based on Questionnaire 2 data. We see that the interpretation

$$F_{22-2} = 76.1 - (1.44) F_{38-1}$$

passes the statistical test line we have used before. This indicates that a linear one-to-one mapping between $F_{22-2}$ and $F_{38-1}$ has some approximate validity. How fruitful is such an indicator of communicability? The factor structures of the two constructs are shown in Table 10.2. The left pole represents a greater score on the factor measure, the right pole a lesser score. The two constructs seem to be, to an outside observer, only moderately related as regards English-language labels. However, it seems probable that there may be very significant associations in reality between companies where "high earnings growth has occurred" and stocks that have "appreciated a great deal recently." What can be seen here are two very different ways of viewing the same, or nearly the same, real-world referent. It is precisely such discoveries that are necessary to facilitate communication. In my view, improper

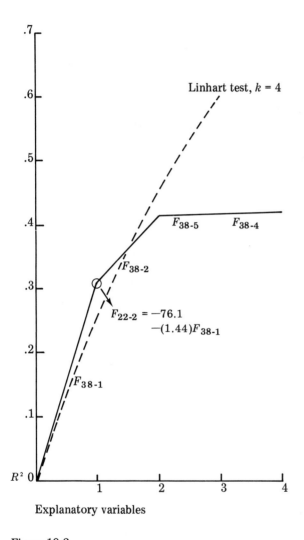

Figure 10.2
Linear Communicability of $F_{22\text{-}2}$ into $F_{38\text{-}1}$, $F_{38\text{-}2}$,
$F_{38\text{-}4}$, and $F_{38\text{-}5}$

Table 10.2
A Comparison of $F_{22\text{-}2}$ and $F_{38\text{-}1}$

| Subject 22, Factor II ($F_{22\text{-}2}$) | |
|---|---|
| .83 demand for final-use products indicates lack of growth | demand for final-use products indicates favorable growth |
| .88 serves consumer market | serves a far from end-use market |
| .82 decline in earnings has occurred | high earnings growth has occurred |
| .77 fortunes tied to factors beyond company's control | not so, research oriented |
| .75 past performance has been worse than expected | past performance has been better than expected |
| .71 in highly competitive business where they are non-unique | in highly specialized market |

| Subject 38, Factor I Reflected ($-F_{38\text{-}1}$) | |
|---|---|
| .88 stock has declined a great deal recently | stock has appreciated a great deal recently |
| .97 presently in market disfavor | is a very fashionable stock at present |
| .87 viewed as a conglomerate | not so |
| .95 closer to its lows than its highs for the year | made new highs for the year very recently |
| .77 cash heavy | not so |

communication is such an important problem that even constructing such modest models may be significant.

The data gathered in Chapter 6 can be used not just to model but rather to re-form attributes and thus assumptions. With these data, the method of canonical correlations may be used to find novel orderings that are the linear aggregates of existing attribute factors and that have best linear mappings between communicants. That is, one can ask the nature of the maximum potential communication between two communicants, given only existing attributes and those formed from linear mappings of these.

Suppose we allow new attribute formations of the following
linear kind:[10]

$$F_1 \text{ (new)} = \Sigma\, \delta_i F_{1j},$$

where $-\infty < \delta < +\infty$. Then clearly Decision-maker 1 can form a
new construct or attribute which can encompass any linear combination of those previously held. Suppose no other kind of attribute formation is allowed, and that the same result holds for
Decision-maker 2. Suppose Decision-makers 1 and 2 attempt the
most perfect communication along any one attribute apiece, and
are allowed to use iteratively a set of common real-world referents
to guide their search for new attributes. Suppose this search con-
tinues until they create a pair of attributes, one for each decision-
maker, which are maximally linearly relatable. Call these two attributes $F_1$ and $F_2$. In my view, canonical correlation techniques
applied to the factor measures created from Questionnaire 1, using
the referents of Questionnaires 2 and 3, hold significant promise
for directly constructing $F_1$ and $F_2$ to shorten this process.[11]

The results of canonical correlation between the two sets of
factor measures and summary preferences from these data for Subjects 22 and 38 is offered as an example. The method extracts first
the best pair of attributes for communication derived from linear
combinations of the two sets of separate variables. Then it extracts
the best remaining pair of attributes for communication of the
remaining variance, etc. The attribute pair's canonical correlation

10. To keep things simple, let us regard each attribute as injective into the
real line.
11. See Anderson (1958) for properties of canonical correlation. Note that
the $Y$ codes based on Questionnaire 3 may be grouped among the $F_k$ for this
purpose, if desirable in the particular application.

Table 10.3.
Pairs of Canonical Variates, Subjects 22 and 38

---

First Pair, Canonical Correlation Coefficient (C.C.) = 0.91
$F_{22} = -(1.44)F_{22\text{-}1} + (0.07)F_{22\text{-}2} - (1.12)F_{22\text{-}3}$
$\quad -(0.52)F_{22\text{-}6} - (0.22)Y_{22}$
$F_{38} = (0.10)F_{38\text{-}1} + (0.69)F_{38\text{-}2} + (0.53)F_{38\text{-}4}$
$\quad -(0.26)F_{38\text{-}5} + (0.18)Y_{38}$

Simplification:
$F_{22} = -F_{22\text{-}1} - F_{22\text{-}3}$
$F_{38} = F_{38\text{-}2} + F_{38\text{-}4}$

Second Pair, C.C. = 0.74
$F_{22} = -(0.87)F_{22\text{-}1} - (1.11)F_{22\text{-}2} - (0.98)F_{22\text{-}3}$
$\quad +(0.24)F_{22\text{-}6} - (0.45)Y_{22}$
$F_{38} = (0.86)F_{38\text{-}1} - (0.14)F_{38\text{-}2} - (0.05)F_{38\text{-}4}$
$\quad -(0.11)F_{38\text{-}5} + (0.36)Y_{38}$

Simplification:
$F_{22} = -F_{22\text{-}1} - F_{22\text{-}2} - F_{22\text{-}3}$
$F_{38} = F_{38\text{-}1}$

---

coefficient is the correlation between the two members of the pair. The results in Table 10.3 give the first and second attribute pairs obtained in this way from the original attribute factors. They were obtained using the canonical correlation computer program in the BMD statistical analysis package. Below each of the full specifications in Table 10.3, a rough simplification is given to focus attention on the main features of each pair. A rather full exploration of the reader's own interpretation of these findings can be made using the factor structures for each subject shown in Appendix C. The second pair of canonical variates is particularly easy to interpret. Taking here the first and *potentially* most communicable pair of canonical variates as a more challenging example, we have

$$F_{22} = -F_{22\text{-}1} - F_{22\text{-}3},$$
$$F_{38} = F_{38\text{-}2} + F_{38\text{-}4}.$$

An inspection of the poles of the four factors yields the following attributes as the opposite poles of a hypothetical superordinate attribute bridging $F_{22}$ and $F_{38}$, shown in Table 10.4. One can imagine a hypothetical superordinate attribute in which these two clusters (as well as their opposites, not shown) would form poles. For example, in a bear market such as prevailed at the time of Questionnaire 2, speculative stocks of new, rapidly growing, but small firms might be technically weak, while large firms or those already out of favor due to fundamental factors might not be so susceptible. The challenge of these results lies in the notion that if

Table 10.4.
Maximally Communicable Linear Hypothetical Construct, Subjects 22 and 38

| (Left Pole from Subject 22) | (Right Pole from Subject 38) |
|---|---|
| From Factor I ($F_{22\text{-}1}$) | From Factor II ($F_{38\text{-}2}$) |
| highly speculative | so vast, beyond comprehension, thus predictable |
| low quality | stock price based on dividends |
| not considerable institutional participation | company less aggressively managing its assets than in the past |
| thin market | old style, sleepy |
| From Factor III ($F_{22\text{-}3}$) | From Factor IV ($F_{38\text{-}4}$) |
| short-term technical demand is weak | |
| long-term technical demand is worsening | |
| short-term technical demand is worsening | presently losing money |
| stock price has recently moved down by a large percentage | |

Subjects 22 and 38 could be led to exercise their imagination in
this way, they could perhaps learn to communicate more effectively.[12]

Still within the framework of simple single assumptions, let us
consider the effect of more fundamental changes in the properties
of the communicants' attribute-ordered sets. In particular, consider the need for one-to-one correspondence between the elements of the two communicants' attributes. In our theory of communication, we have assumed that corresponding pairs of members
refer to *the same* real-world object or referent. Clearly, what one
means by *the same* real-world referent is somewhat ambiguous
here. However, intuitively, the more real-world objects that are
experientially shared and categorized as to attribute position by
the communicants, the greater the possibility of nearly perfect
one-to-one correspondence between those attributes. This does
not imply that the attributes be similar. It does imply that each
event or object categorized by one communicant will also be categorized by the other. This inducement of shared real-world referents is directly promoted by the activity of Questionnaire 2. Thus,
not only is Questionnaire 2 data helpful in mapping correspondences between attributes, it also helps to ensure that there *are*
correspondences.

Thus the extension of each attribute to include new referents
involves in itself a subtle alteration of the attribute structure of
the decision-maker. To see the benefits of this activity, imagine
the communication problems of an over-the-counter trader who
deals only with new issues and a bank trust officer who deals only

12. They might also be stimulated to construct new attributes more useful in
decision-making. The situation is rather analogous to the advantage of sexual
reproduction over asexual reproduction in speeding up evolution and providing for adaptability.

with seasoned issues of wide marketability. Unless at least one of these two can be led to extend his conceptual structure to include the other's referents, there may be limited possibility for a meaningful translation of ideas between them.

**Value-Laden Communication**

The foregoing difficulties of so-called "objective" or "value free" communication are dwarfed as compared to those of communications that assume shared decision assumptions. Clearly, however, the measures of decision assumptions obtained in Chapter 6 and shown in Appendix D offer a great aid to interpreting messages such as, "that is a good stock," or better yet, "that is a good stock for long-term capital gains." Instinctively, we rely on the value-laden statements of others only when we are confident they share our assumptions. Conversely, we try to enforce commonality of decision assumptions so we can realize the efficiencies of value-laden communication. Both these necessities are reduced by explicit decision assumption measurement. The more knowledge one has of the other's decision assumptions, the more effectively one can decode his value judgments. In a world of varied training, culture, and ideologies, this may significantly enlarge our sources of useful information. That is, it makes it more possible to learn from those with whom one does not agree.

## 10.3. Use of Decision Assumptions Where Ongoing Cooperation Is Not Assumed

In Chapter 1, a number of practical problems analogous to those arising in marketing research were raised. The distinguishing features of such problems are that one decision-maker needs to know more about the decisions of another decision-maker who is not involved in ongoing cooperation with the first. In practice, this usually implies greater uncertainty regarding his assumptions. It also implies either indifference or active opposition to being measured.

In such cases, there is a relatively high payoff for explicit attacks on measuring decision assumptions, and particularly on discovering the relevant attributes. This is probably why the practical application of such techniques is much further advanced in marketing and political opinion research than in the applications previously described.

The method of measurement outlined in this book is not well suited for measurement where the decision-maker is strongly hostile to the measurer.[13] On the other hand, its relatively inexpensive procedure and the mildly projective nature of its initial Role Repertory Test make it well suited for marketing and political opinion research.

Suppose one is attempting to prepare suitable advertising for a product or publicity for a political candidate. Obviously, the decision assumption measures of Chapter 6 when applied to the customer or voter will indicate relevant attributes on which to channel one's message. Alternatively, suppose one is attempting to outline the appropriate characteristics as inputs to designing a new product or nominating a new candidate (or modifying old ones) most appealing to a given homogeneous class of decision-makers. Clearly, the same models of decision assumptions can give useful hints.[14]

When marketing to a number of customers whose decision assumptions are not homogeneous, however, a modified approach may be useful. In this situation, one constructs a map of the

13. Even in these cases, the use of a representative surrogate decision-maker who has been specially compensated may make this measure feasible, however.

14. See Lunn (1969) and Morgan and Purnell (1969).

competitor products or candidates in an attribute space based on aggregated data. Then, as a heuristic, one looks for openings or empty regions in the space. A new product will have little competition within such a region. Thus any customers who prefer that region highly will constitute a stable, well-defined, and readily obtainable market. Even when it is necessary to expand one's appeal to more contested regions of the attribute space, as in two-party politics, such a map can be made useful by projecting onto it the "ideal points" of the various decision-makers.[15] This will indicate the possibilities for inserting one's own product between a competitor's position and the central moment of the ideal points of the necessary quantity of the decision-makers. In such applications, the use of the truly relevant attributes in constructing the spatial map is a key influence on success.

Such procedures of new product and new policy or candidate design may remain partly an art. However, it is already clear that they will in the future be profoundly influenced by explicit assumption measurement techniques.

The applications of this chapter are generally less familiar and will require more implementation research than those for the individual decision-maker described earlier. Our approach to aggregate decision-making and to communication may prove more interesting to academicians than to managers for some time to come. In market research, however, which has already seen considerable work of this sort, sophisticated practical applications are a reality.

It is difficult to overestimate the importance of the use of more precise assumption measures, and set-theoretic notions in which to embed them, for the progress of the theory of economics and political science. In Chapter 3, various axioms of the microeco-

15. See the discussion of ideal points in Chapter 8.

nomic model were noted in passing. One of the chief tasks for future theory appears to be to demonstrate how certain mechanisms for combining individual decisions that do not conform to these axioms may produce aggregate decisions that *do* so conform. This theoretical progress will be aided by accompanying empirical measurements.

In sociology, which is generally in a somewhat more primitive state, the ultimate impact of more precise measures for measuring the development and communication of social ideas is also likely to be extensive.

In the next chapter, these theoretical implications are discussed further.

**In Summary**

Very often the decision assumptions of a number of individuals with different backgrounds need to be coordinated. This is true in joint, or aggregate, decision-making; it is true in communication; it is true in market or opinion research.

Through explicit separation of the various attributes that go into complex assumptions, it is in my view possible to improve greatly the potential effectiveness of aggregation of disparate viewpoints in joint decision-making. At a still more basic level, it is possible to use such explicit measures together with common referents to improve communication along existing attributes and to develop more communicable attributes. In this chapter, methods for improving aggregate decision-making and communication were illustrated in the context of my study of stock market participants. In addition, methods for more precise market or opinion research were described briefly.

## 11

Decision Assumption
Measurement — Implications
for Social Science

In this chapter and the next, some hypotheses are discussed regarding what one might do to advance the social sciences with the present method of measuring decision assumptions. I regard such methods as important tools not only for immediate practical application but also for the construction and empirical testing of aspects of social science theory.

In this chapter, indications for research in the fields of psychology, organization theory, political science, economics, and sociology are sketched. I do not presume special competence in these fields. The remarks that follow are suggestions intended to ensnare the interest of the reader looking for a new tool to use in attacking his own scientific problems.

## 11.1. Individual Psychology

It is perhaps stretching a point to regard cognitive psychology as one of the social sciences. Yet, the nature of high-order cognitive functioning is indisputably pertinent to important social phenomena. Measurement of decision assumptions can give strong signals as to styles of cognitive functioning. I believe these signals may well be used to understand better the nature of scientific and managerial skills, many of the determinants of mental and personality disorders, and more effective educational procedures.

Of course, these beliefs have been influenced by the great depth and variety of relevant work in the field of psychology. There is some evidence from this work that each decision-maker employs similar styles of cognitive functioning across broad areas of different decisions he makes. At the same time, work in trait testing has led to increased knowledge as to the use of decision assumptions in decision-making and as to the processes by which they are

formed. For example, studies in cognitive control processes (Gardner, Jackson, and Messick 1960), information processing capacity
(Streufert and Driver 1965), concept learning (Hovland and Weiss
1953; Bruner, Goodnow, and Austin 1957; Glanzer, Buttenlocher,
and Clark 1963), and planning styles (Danziger and Morsbach
1967) provide many useful insights into the relationship between
cognitive styles and activity. These studies, in fact, were major
motivations toward the present research in measuring assumptions.

Many studies in this area have related quantifiable characteristics of cognitive assumptions to decision-making styles. These
characteristics include such variables as the number of underlying
attribute dimensions, the polarization of objects classified within
attributes, and the complexity of organization of the attributes to
form concepts. That is, some further links have been provided
between attribute characteristics and the way decision assumptions relate to the subject's activity (Sherif and Hovland 1953;
Bieri 1955; Pettigrew 1958; Triandis 1959; Scott 1962; Messick
and Kogan 1963; Runkel 1963; Bruner and Tajfel 1965; Glixman
1965; Phares and Davis 1966; Rotter and Rotter 1966; Francher
1970; Robinson and Hefner 1967; Taylor and Haygood 1968).

All of the specific characteristics cited in this literature can be
measured using the method of this book. For example, within the
context of a given field of different objects, one can measure the
number of attribute factors used to categorize these objects and
how their use is distributed, using data from Questionnaire 1.[1] On
each attribute, one can measure discrimination by an entropy
quantity $(H)$ over the content equivalence intervals, or just by
counting the number of intervals. Note that $H = -\sum_i p_i \log p_i$,
where $p_i$ is the probability of an object being categorized in the $i$th

1. See Chapter 5.

interval. Within each attribute one could observe consistent tendencies for objects to be categorized with a central peak (low polarity) or double peak (high polarity). The analysis of the decision assumptions based on Questionnaires 2 and 3 could give further potentially useful indicators of cognitive style. For example, consistency of assumptions over time might be an interesting signal. Along this line, one could better measure the relative impact of new information as opposed to noise on the cognitive structure of the individual. Resulting individual differences in response to dissonant new data might yield new understanding for advancing the theory of cognitive dissonance.[2]

Two efforts in individual psychology which deserve special mention are those by George Kelly and H. M. Schroder.

Kelly's massive book, The *Psychology of Personal Constructs*, outlines a theory of personality which stresses the importance of consistent patterns of perception and decision assumptions in determining personality characteristics.[3] Many of the variables in his theory would benefit from the improved empirical measures derivable from methods like the one of this book. For example, his variable, *permeability* of constructs (attributes), could be measured using the "scale not relevant" interval. Effective applications of his theory and improvements of the theory might be enhanced by such better empirical measures. Parenthetically, his theory of the role of the therapist in helping the patient learn new constructs might well be keenly relevant to more conventional educational psychology.

2. See Festinger (1962). The theory of cognitive dissonance has apparently become unfashionable because of the lack of such a tie to more precise empirical data.
3. See Kelly (1955). Permeability refers to the ability of attributes to assimilate new objects.

The work of H. M. Schroder and his associates has focused on decision-making effectiveness as a function of information processing work load and cognitive structuring capability. They have been particularly interested in cognitive complexity. This refers to the number, and complexity of organization, of attributes making up the concepts used by the decision-maker. I take Schroder's notion of a "concept" to be equivalent to a segment of a decision net which forms a sufficiently well knit whole to serve as a generalizable module. That is, it can readily be integrated as a whole into new decision nets with minor modification of internal structure. This is also equivalent to Piaget's "schema."[4]

The method of the present book forms a logical extension of those methods already used by Schroder in carrying out empirical studies of determinants of information processing capability. The extension to measuring decision assumptions, rather than just attribute use, offers particularly new potential for tracing out the manner in which attributes are combined to form concepts.

## 11.2. Social Psychology and Organization Theory[5]

One can loosely structure this area into theories of dyads, face-to-face or primary groups, and theories of organizations of interrelated primary groups.

Among the more interesting aspects of dyads are the nature of the forces that hold them together. There may be some evidence that the most favorable conditions for marriage, for example, are similarity of culture but differences in personality. A risky but interesting hypothesis is that the members of successful dyads use

4. See Schroder (1967); see Piaget (1959).
5. See Lindzey (1968).

broadly similar attributes but differ in the particular cognitive styles with which they use them. This hypothesis could be tested with explicit measures of decision assumptions in a task area of important mutual decision-making for the marriage couple. Of course, task characteristics might have an important influence on the most desirable balance.

Two important variables in the theory of primary groups are those of *cohesiveness* and *strength of group norms*. One would suspect that both these variables were positively related to homogeneity of decision assumptions across the group members, based either on prior background or shared group experience. Another interesting phenomenon is the apparent dependence of group communication volume directed toward a group member on the degree of his deviance from group norms. This apparently rises with a slight deviance of the member from group norms, but falls as the deviance becomes more pronounced. These phenomena could all be more precisely explored with explicit measures of decision assumptions.

An issue of more than passing interest in the theory of hierarchical organizations is how the objectives of those in power get transformed as they percolate their way down to the personnel at the operating level. One might obtain insights into this process and into the consistency of the results by estimating the transformation between hierarchical levels of attributes used in characterizing the same real-world problem referents.[6]

The method of this book could be an important tool for workers in the field of sociometry. In this field, one measures the

6. This application was suggested to the author by Z. Zannetos in a private communication. See also Zannetos (1965).

interpersonal similarities in likes and dislikes. Using these data, one constructs a map of clusters of individuals. These clusters sometimes reveal a great deal about the internal structure of organizations. Factor analysis, cluster analysis, and multidimensional scaling methods can be used here.

As an example, the subjects' preference data from Questionnaire 3 in the stock market study were factor analyzed. The results are shown in Table 11.1. The individual decision-makers are taken as the variables. The results of this analysis do a remarkable job in distinguishing among decision-makers of differing organizational ties. That is, decision-makers within an organization tended to have highly correlated preferences. This kind of analysis could be used to study patterns of organizational homogeneity of preferences or decision assumptions. Of course, much more sophisti-

Table 11.1.
Cross-Subject Factor Structure

| Factor I | | | Factor II | | |
|---|---|---|---|---|---|
| Subject | Loading | Organization | Subject | Loading | Organization |
| 03 | .89 | Trust A | 23 | .81 | Individual |
| 04 | .79 | Trust A | 24 | .72 | Trust A* |
| 05 | .71 | Trust A | 27 | .81 | Trust B |
| 07 | .84 | Trader | 28 | .90 | Trust B |
| 13 | .69 | Fund A | 30 | .73 | Trust B |
| 15 | .80 | Fund C | 31 | .75 | Trust B |
| 17 | .80 | Individual | 35 | .66 | Trust B |
| 19 | .86 | Individual | | | |
| 22 | .90 | Individual | | | |
| 26 | .73 | Trust B | | | |
| 37 | .66 | Trust A | | | |
| 38 | .74 | Fund A | | | |

Note: Some of the research done by Trust A was utilized by Fund A.

* This subject resigned his position during the course of the study.

cated analyses of sociometric configurations could be made using the attribute factor ratings.[7]

## 11.3. Political Science, Economics, and Sociology

### Political Science

One of the most interesting questions facing the field of political science today is the nature of the specific characteristics of various political mechanisms in terms of the manner in which they aggregate individual preferences to obtain group decisions. Work in this area may ultimately have significant, perhaps a decisive, influence on the course of the social sciences. The current approach to this area is in the realm of abstract mathematics.[8] A complementary approach that might be much aided by the method expounded in this book is empirical research. That is, one could obtain individual ratings of decision alternatives as to attributes and preferences. A particular mechanism, such as, for example, discussion and voting under Robert's Rules of Order, could be used to establish group decisions. Then one could empirically explore the question of the extent to which such a process is amenable to a topologically convenient choice-set representation. Another hypothesis for testing is whether the final output could be predicted by such a representation based not on attributes used by individuals but by constructed attributes obtained by pooling individual data. Incidentally, such questions underlie the experiment by Green and Maheshwari in which individual data were pooled, as discussed in Chapter 8.

7. This analysis, however, requires the development of improved methods of aggregation of individual attribute data. The author is currently exploring the use of weighted factor analysis of the factor scores derived from the individual decision-maker factor analyses.
8. See Arrow and Debreu (1954), Tullock (1967).

The results of this research could be very valuable in better understanding the operating characteristics of political institutions.

**Economics**

As far back as fifty years ago, some thoughtful economists suggested the importance of economic actors' conceptual structures in determining economic behavior. For example, Mitchell (1910) pondered the nature of economic rationality:

> . . . a modern child is offered, ready-made, a vast assortment of mental tools [concepts] with which to perform his tasks. . . . With this saving of effort there goes a marked standardization of thinking and acting. . . . the concepts supply the basis for rationality. . . . their acquisition trains the individual in reflection [and] marks out the lines of his own planning. . . . [Social concepts'] daily use by all members of a social group unremittingly molds these individuals into common patterns without their knowledge. . . .

This kind of thinking did not proceed very far, however, until the rise of econometrics and dynamic model building. When economists attempted not just to explain but to predict dynamic economic behavior, they found new variables were needed.

In an article of fundamental importance, F. A. von Hayek (1937) discussed the implications of relaxing the micro- and macroeconomic assumptions of perfect knowledge. He argued that it was the dynamic flow of imperfect knowledge which was basic to nontrivial behavior, and it was this process which theory should model. Shortly thereafter, Sweezy (1938) argued for the specific admission of imperfect *expectations* as variables in economic models.

Thus began a steady increase of interest within the literature of economics regarding expectations (Lachmann 1943; Shackle 1943; von Hayek 1942, 1943, 1944, 1945; Katona 1947). Today, the inclusion of business expectations as an explanatory variable in

macroeconomic models is almost routine. However, expectations
as empirical dependent variables proved not so tractable. Lachmann, in particular, noted a major difficulty:

> ... the absence of a uniform relationship between a set of observ-
> able events which might be described as a *situation* on the one
> hand, and expectations on the other hand, is ... the crux of the
> whole matter. Expectations, it is true, are largely a response to
> events experienced in the past, but the *modus operandi* of the
> response is not the same in all cases even of the same experience.
> ... The next step in the study of expectations has to consist of
> evolving hypothetical 'ideal types' and testing them in the light of
> economic history. ... But it cannot be emphasized too strongly
> that if these efforts were to be confined to the study of relations
> between objective facts and expectations they would be quite use-
> less. The Social World consists not of facts but of our interpreta-
> tions of the facts. ... we are here facing a fundamental issue in the
> methodology of economics. ... [9]

Lachmann's view has been quoted at length because it represents one of the principal issues of the present research, and it
remains a major jumping-off point from the field of economics
toward the explicit measurement of decision assumptions sought
here. Thus far, economists have been extremely cautious in taking
account of the effect of variant subjective interpretations of the
same objective situations.

Clearly, a major reason why the observer may not see a uniform
relationship between a set of observable events and the resulting
expectations is that the observer may be using different attributes
than the decision-maker. This particular stumbling block may be
attacked and overcome through the application of the measurement method of this book. A second obstacle to economists has
been the use of aggregate data. Its need depends in part on the
practical feasibility of alternative, individually oriented methods.

9. See L. M. Lachmann (1943), on the role of expectations in economics.

A third, and fundamental, obstacle is the imperfection of a choice-set representation approach in modeling certain decision nets.[10] The present method offers only the opportunity to better ascertain the true extent of this obstacle by winnowing out the problems just discussed.

Economists might well be interested also in determining the characteristics of various groups of economic actors of special economic interest. For example, do good entrepreneurs have distinct assumptions regarding solutions to business problems? What are the assumptions of consumers regarding the influence of correlates of macroeconomic variables on consumer spending? Attempts to answer such questions would benefit from better methods of modeling decision-maker assumptions.

**Sociology**

The sociological work following the path set by Karl Mannheim has been known as the sociology of knowledge.[11] This approach analyzes interclass and international interactions in terms of the practical ideology of different groups. For example, one can predict social revolutions on the basis of the rise of an ideology conflicting with that previously dominant. The applications suggested earlier for sociometry may also be used for measuring particular decision assumptions that play a key role in ideologies.

It seems likely such an improved tool for measuring interideological differences and charting their slow evolution under the impact of events would put this field on a much stronger footing. In a practical sense, such an advance would also contribute greatly to our ability to really understand foreign affairs.

10. Again, see Simon (1959).
11. See Mannheim (1962). See also an analysis of the Soviet view of education in Kelly (1962).

## In Summary

Development of the social sciences requires not only better theories but also proper instruments for the measurement of theoretical variables. It is hard to conceive of the development of thermodynamics without the invention of the thermometer. I take the view that appropriate characterization of the interrelationship of individual decision assumptions and aggregate, social decision assumptions will prove to be fundamental to the development of a general social science. Thus, in the same way, it is hard to conceive of this advance without good measuring instruments for individual decision assumptions.

The method offered in this book is undoubtedly subject to improvement. Yet it seems to offer increased feasibility for specific studies in the various branches of social science which would contribute to this overall goal. The indications in this chapter for studies in psychology, organization theory, economics, political science, and sociology are mere suggestions. The reader engaged in social science research can formulate his own applications without much trouble.

In the next chapter, applications are sketched for accounting and the study of financial markets. These are specifically relatable to my study of stock market participants. Despite their narrow focus, they are nonetheless valid examples of the kinds of research which will lead to better understanding of the role of markets in aggregating individual decision assumptions to produce social decisions.

# 12

This chapter deals with applications suggested by the stock market participant study reported earlier.

## 12.1 The Subjective Information of Accounting Reports for Investors

The profession of accounting seeks to present measures of business performance to external decision-makers. Of these, one of the most important classes is the investor. How are accounting reports used by the investor? How could they be made more useful?

Research regarding the information content of accounting data as reflected in changes in stock prices has mainly indicated the apparent short-term influence of changes in earnings. There are two major drawbacks to such studies for answering our rhetorical questions, however. First, much of the change in stock prices correlated with accounting data occurs *before* the actual accounting report is issued. Second, the effects of long-run patterns of accounting report figures have not been investigated.

The first drawback means that we cannot easily differentiate the effect of changes in specific near-term expectations regarding reported accounting figures from more general changes in the investor's image of the firm's management or situation. For example, subjective impressions of long-run managerial ability may well be somewhat correlated with immediate changes in earnings. However it is important to know if investors rely directly on near-term reported earnings as a variable in determining their preferences, or if such reported earnings are merely one component measure or partial surrogate for more general concepts underlying long-term profitability.

Examples of these underlying variables may be managerial ability or product growth prospects. If reported earnings are surrogate for these, it may be plausible to improve the flow of information to investors through additional data on new products and management in the annual and quarterly reports. If not, however, the main source of improvement would have to come through more frequent reporting and refinement in the measurement of income. The implications for the accounting profession are quite different in the two cases. In particular, more frequent reporting means more arbitrary allocations of income over time and thus means greater pressures on the accountant who certifies the reports.

The second drawback, the lack of study of the effect on long-term patterns in accounting figures, suggests that additional research is needed to make wise policy judgments regarding accounting practices that "smooth" reported income versus those that tend to show a rising pattern followed by an unpleasant surprise.

Both these drawbacks could be better overcome if we had access to some intermediate variables — the subjective impressions of investors regarding firms. These impressions are interposed between the accounting reports and the investor's stock market behavior. Such variables could be correlated with investor preferences on the one hand, and both short- and long-term patterns of accounting data, on the other hand, to produce a more useful picture of how accounting data are used.

As a result of decision assumption measurement of stock market participants, these subjective data are already available. They could be gathered on a larger scale using the method of this book or any similar method for explicitly measuring the assumptions of decision-makers.

A potentially rewarding research project in this area might consist of an empirical test of the existence of relationships between major accounting report data variables such as earnings and sales and the attribute ratings gathered in Questionnaire 2 of the stock market study. Various statistical methods might be used, but simple multivariate regression could be the basic tool. Among the tests there could be two key parts. First, one could conduct a statistical regression of measures of long-term patterns of earnings growth and steadiness against subjective impressions and preferences. Second, a similar study could be done relating short-term accounting report figures, especially changes in earnings, to the short-term changes in the subjective impressions and preferences recorded between two separate measures of decision assumptions over time.

The fundamental opportunity offered is for improved understanding of how accounting reports are used by the investor. It is not easy to make wise judgments as to reporting practices most useful to the investor without very extensive knowledge in this area. The frames of reference within which investors interpret accounting data may not correspond very closely to academic and professional accounting viewpoints. Only empirical studies linking objective accounting data with investor's subjective attributes will bridge the gap.

Also, in such studies data should be gathered indicating the extent to which any managerial manipulation of accounting reports might be expected to sway investors' opinions. This also may be helpful in determining appropriate guidelines for acceptable accounting practices.

## 12.2. Research on the General Characteristics of Markets and on the Stock Market

In conducting the previously reported study of stock market participants it became obvious that the method used could help in answering certain questions about the market which have long been of interest to the field of finance.

The existing theory of capital markets has produced two results of fundamental importance. First, average returns to investors cannot be improved, at a given risk, by trading rules based on the same information generally available to other investors.[1] Second, possibilities of arbitrage and diversification of risk for the investor assure that expected returns to individual securities will, on the average, conform fairly closely to a simple capital asset pricing model.[2]

Both these results heavily rely on a particular simplification in the model of investor behavior. They presume that investors interpret new information in the same way, and differ only in risk preferences.[3] The present study of stock market participants shows very clearly the heroic nature of this supposition. Investors differ, sometimes very dramatically, in the way they interpret new information.

The random walk and capital asset pricing results might be subtly different if based on a model incorporating nonhomogeneous investor assumptions. A reasonable conjecture is that in the limit as numbers of different types of investors are increased, the capital asset pricing models would converge. On the other hand, for smaller numbers of different types of investors, the answer is not so obvious.[4]

1. This is the random walk theory. See Cootner (1964) for an early review of the literature in this area.
2. See Markowitz (1952), and Jensen (1970).
3. See Section 3.1.
4. This problem is roughly analogous to microeconomic theories of monopoly, oligopoly, and perfect competition. It is the middle case that is difficult, ultimately requiring a game-theoretic treatment.

Since empirical results indicate the fairly close, though not exact, fits of the random walk and capital asset pricing models, our present concern may appear superfluous. This may not be the case, however. As large institutional investors more and more dominate the market, the effective number of different types of investors might well decrease. It is possible that we may then experience some of that middle ground with which present financial theory probably does not deal adequately. Thus, further theoretical work using a small number of "ideal types" of investors would be very helpful. This could determine whether particular types of government regulation of the securities markets is necessary to preserve their desirable properties as nearly perfect markets. The contribution of the present work is in terms of empirical evidence on which to base particular models of "ideal types" of various kinds of investor decision processes.

A subissue relatively easy to approach is the extent of destabilizing investor assumptions. One would expect that assumptions such as "if the stock has been *rising* then *buy*" would have a tendency to be destabilizing. It may be critical to effective market regulation to know the relative activity and financial power of investors of this type as opposed to those who feel the opposite, or even as opposed to those who feel that "if a stock is *high* in relation to earnings then *sell*."

A rather different kind of study, but in some ways the dual of the first, is an exploration of "ideal types" of *stocks*. Individual investors have a fairly clear feeling for which stocks are similar with respect to their own assumptions. Relatively few, however, appear to have a clear perception of similarities among stocks with respect to the way other investors view them. These latter similarities would be of use not only in the accounting research proposed in the previous section but also in practical affairs such as effective underwriting and perhaps even in investing.

As an illustration of a simple approach to understanding these similarities, the preference data gathered in Questionnaire 5 were factor analyzed. This time, the individual stocks were used as variables. The results are shown in Table 12.1. Of course, more sophisticated structures could be obtained with the factor attribute scores of Questionnaire 4, but with greater difficulty.

Readers who have participated actively in the stock market will find Factors I, III, V, and VI easy to interpret. The factors tell us

Table 12.1.
Stock Factor Structure of Questionnaire 5 Preferences, November 1969.

| Factor I | Factor II |
|---|---|
| .53 City Investing | .73 AMF |
| .82 Fairchild Camera | .79 Chrysler |
| .70 LTV | −.73 Delta Airlines |
| .57 Texas Instruments | .68 ITT |
|  | .52 Std. Oil of New Jersey |
|  | .51 Texas Instruments |
| **Factor III** | **Factor IV** |
| .83 Bethlehem Steel | .75 Control Data |
| .77 Massey Ferguson | .64 Std. Oil of Indiana |
| .79 Monsanto | .68 Std. Oil of New Jersey |
|  | −.64 Varian Associates |
| **Factor V** | **Factor VI** |
| .64 Four Seasons Nursing Centers | .62 Digital Equipment |
| .86 Pacific Petroleum | .77 Polaroid |
| .79 Simon & Schuster |  |

Note: The standard error of each loading is estimated at 0.3

that, for example, the same investors who preferred Fairchild Camera tended to prefer LTV, and vice versa. Also, those who liked Delta Airlines did not like Chrysler, etc.

### 12.3. Normative Implications for Investor Behavior

The capital asset pricing model of financial theory suggests average investor returns conform closely to the returns that can be expected by buying stocks at random from a given risk class and holding them for long periods.

The investor may either content himself with such average returns or try to obtain extraordinary returns. In the first case, his task is relatively simple. He can get good results by random selection within a risk class. The average risk associated with a stock can be fairly well estimated from its past degree of volatility as compared with the market as a whole. In the second case, however, his task is much more difficult. He must invalidate the assumptions of the capital asset pricing model in his instance. He can do this either by gaining *inside access* to information before it is available to the market, or else by becoming an investor with a point of view different than those already expressed in the market. That is, unless he is an insider, having a different point of view than is held widely by other market participants is a necessary condition of his valid expectation of extraordinary gains. Unfortunately, it is not a sufficient condition.

Still, the methods outlined in Chapter 9 are well suited for the discovery of useful new ways of interpreting data and even of new attributes to incorporate in investor assumptions. They are complemented by the application of the ideas discussed in Section 10.3 in determining the assumptions of the market with which one must differ to obtain extraordinary returns.

Of course, the activities of investors in seeking such new insights have a tendency to make the market more perfect and more intelligent in the long run.

## In Summary

Accountants have increasingly concerned themselves with the impact of accounting methods on investors. To my knowledge, however, most of the data available have been restricted to market security prices. These data reflect aggregated assumptions without revealing the process of aggregation. They do not furnish as much illumination toward guidelines for improving accounting reports as would data on individual decision-maker information usage.

On a different front, in the last decade the development of better theories for understanding capital asset pricing in markets and the random character of arrival of new information to the market has increased our awareness of the role of financial markets in our society. The empirical support for this work is based on market security prices. The theory, however, deals partly with the decision assumptions of individuals. Except for risk preferences, these individuals are presumed to have homogeneous decision assumptions. The stock market participant study reported here shows the heroic nature of this presumption.[5] Better theories will account for empirically observable security price data in terms of aggregates of inhomogeneous investor decision assumptions. The construction of such theories would be stimulated, in my

5. Of course, the finance academician's first line of defense will be that the apparent differences among investors are just differences in labels for risk and return. This question deserves further study.

opinion, by consideration of "ideal types" of individual decision assumptions.

Both accounting and financial market theory would thus be well served by more research linking objective accounting and other business data to subjective market participant impressions along their own, peculiar attributes through their assumptions and thence to the behavior of security prices.

Finally, I offer a word of advice to the ambitious market participant. If he hopes to entertain a reasonable expectation of above-average returns at a given risk level, it is necessary to invalidate the presumptions of the capital asset price model in his case. Either he must secure pertinent data unavailable to other participants, or he must develop a point of view not yet represented in the market. Judging by my own study, negotiating either path is indeed an arduous task, requiring both unusual creativity and precision of method.

# Appendixes

**Appendix A**                         Derivation of Factor Measure
                                      Transforms


The data from the first questionnaire were factor analyzed in order to derive a transform that could then be applied to fresh data from succeeding questionnaires. Since the estimated factor structure was itself a small-sample observation, the resulting transform was imperfect compared to that which might be derivable from the population factor structure. However, the knowledge thus brought to bear, though imperfect, was distinctly useful; by reducing the number of explanatory variables, it made possible regression models upon which one could place some confidence. A maximum of three factor measure variables (quasi factor scores) was used in regression models based on twenty observations.

The derivation of the transforms may be expressed mathematically as follows. The exposition follows Harman (1967). We have

$$Z = AF,$$

where $A$ represents the $n \times m$ matrix of principal component loadings, with $n$ variables and $m$ factors, $Z$ the $n \times n'$ matrix of raw data attributes normalized to zero mean and unit variance, with $n'$ observations, and $F$ the $m \times n'$ matrix of hypothesized principal component scores. In addition, we have obtained loadings for rotated factors $B$ and corresponding rotated factor scores $G$, where $B = AT$ and $T$ is an orthogonal transformation matrix. Thus, $Z = AF$ and $Z = BG$, where $B = AT$. None of the foregoing matrices need be square. We desire an estimate of $G$, given $Z, A, B$, and also given $\Lambda$, a diagonal matrix of the eigenvalues $\lambda_k$, $(k = 1, \ldots, m)$ of the matrix $A$. We know from the theory of matrices and factor analysis that $T'\,T = I$ and $A'\,A = A$ Thus we have

$$BG = AF, \text{ since both equal } Z;$$
$$ATG = AF,$$

$TG = F$,
$T'TG = T'F$,
$G = T'F$, since $T'T = I$.

Now we want to find known expressions for $F$ and then for $T'$. Since

$Z = AF$,

we have

$A'AF = A'Z$.

We do not want to invert $A$, which may not be square; thus,

$F = (A'A)^{-1} A'Z$.

Combining, we have

$G = T'(A'A)^{-1} A'Z$.

Finally, using

$B = AT$

we can find $T'$. We have

$A'AT = A'B$,
$\quad T = (A'A)^{-1} A'B$,
$\quad T' = [(A'A)^{-1} A'B]'$.

Combining all terms, we have

$G = [(A'A)^{-1}A'B]' (A'A)^{-1}A'Z$,
$\quad = B'A [(A'A)^{-1}]' (A'A)^{-1}A'Z$
$\quad = B'A [A'A]^{-2}A'Z$, since $(A'A)^{-1} = [(A'A)^{-1}]'$
$\quad = [B'A\Lambda^{-2}A']Z$, since $A'A = \Lambda$.

The final term in brackets is a matrix that can be used to transform a new data set to quasi factor scores; it requires knowledge only of **B**, **A**, and $\Lambda$, and requires only simple matrix multiplication and transposition to calculate (since $\Lambda$ is diagonal, its inverse is just the matrix whose diagonal elements are the reciprocals of the elements of $\Lambda$).

This exact transform can often be closely approximated using only the first few columns of A, B, and $\Lambda$. In practice $m = n$ is typical, but we approximate the analysis using a smaller number of components.

Appendix B                    Sample Questionnaires and
                              Interview Materials


This appendix gives page references to places in the main text where sample materials are shown. Also, some additional questionnaire samples of points not emphasized in the main text are given. The following headings are contained:

1. Description of materials and procedures used for interview
2. Two examples of lists of stocks elicited from subjects in the interview
3. A sample transcription from an interview tape recording
4. Sample notes taken while listening to tape-recorded interviews
5. Questionnaire 1, instructions and typical response
6. Two typical subjects' responses to Questionnaire 2
7. Instructions to Questionnaire 3
8. Two typical subjects' responses to Questionnaire 3
9. List of stocks used for Questionnaires 2 and 3
10. List of stocks used for Questionnaires 4 and 5


**1. Interview Materials and Procedures**
See pages 68 through 71 in the text.


**2. Example Individual Lists of Stocks**
See page 70.


**3. Sample Interview Tape-Recording Transcription**
See pages 72 through 73.


**4. Sample Notes from Listening to Tape Recordings**
See pages 74 through 75.


**5. Questionnaire 1, Instructions and Typical Response**
See pages 75 through 77.

## 6. Two Typical Subjects' Responses to Questionnaire 2

In Table B.1 are given the first five raw attribute scales obtained from Subject 26, a trust officer who was successfully modeled. In Table B.2 are given corresponding data from Subject 39, an individual investor who was *not* well modeled.

The reader should note that, reflecting the differences in Questionnaire 1, each subject received his own individualized version of

Table B.1.
First Five Attribute Scales for Subject 26

|  |  |  |  |  |  |  | Q. no. | 2 |
|--|--|--|--|--|--|--|--------|---|
|  |  |  |  |  |  |  | S. no. | 26 |

**1.**

| 6 | 14, 18 | 9, 16 | 4, 7 | | 10, 11 | 5, 8 | 20 |
|---|--------|-------|------|--|--------|------|----|
| glamour growth stock | | | | | | | not so |

| | 1, 2, 13, 15, 17 | 3, 12, 19 |
|--|------------------|-----------|
| | Scale does not apply | Not enough information |

**2.**

| 1, 9, 10, 11, 14, 15, 16, 17, 18, 20 | 2, 4, 5, 7, 13 | 6, 8 |
|--------------------------------------|----------------|------|
| high quality | | low quality |

| | | 3, 12, 19 |
|--|--|-----------|
| | Scale does not apply | Not enough information |

**3.**

| 9, 14, 15, 16 | 5, 6, 10, 11, 18, 20 | 1, 2, 4, 7, 8 |
|---------------|----------------------|---------------|
| has demonstrated a good progression of earnings for a number of years | | not so |

| | | 3, 12, 19, 13, 17 |
|--|--|-------------------|
| | Scale does not apply | Not enough information |

Table B.1. (cont.)
First Five Attribute Scales for Subject 26

| 4. | 2, 4, 5, 6, 7, 8, 9, 13, 20 | 14, 15, 16, 17, 18 | 1, 10, 11 |
|---|---|---|---|
| | has been an exceptional stock performer | | has been an unexceptional performer |

| | | | 3, 12, 19 |
|---|---|---|---|
| | | Scale does not apply | Not enough information |

| 5. | 3, 4, 5, 6, 7, 9, 12, 14, 17, 18, 20 | 8, 13, 16 | 1, 2, 10, 11, 15 |
|---|---|---|---|
| | involved in a stock market fad | | not so |

| | | | 19 |
|---|---|---|---|
| | | Scale does not apply | Not enough information |

Table B.2.
First Five Attribute Scales for Subject 39.

|  |  | Q. no. | 2 |
|---|---|---|---|
|  |  | S. no. | 39 |

| 1. | 5 | 15 | rest |
|---|---|---|---|
| | recommended by a person in whom I have confidence | | not so |

| | | Scale does not apply | Not enough information |
|---|---|---|---|

| 2. | | 15, 16, 17, 18, 19, 20<br>1, 2, 5, 7, 9, 10, 11, 12, 14 |
|---|---|---|
| | recent new issue | has been traded for many years |

| | | | 3, 4, 6, 8, 13 |
|---|---|---|---|
| | | Scale does not apply | Not enough information |

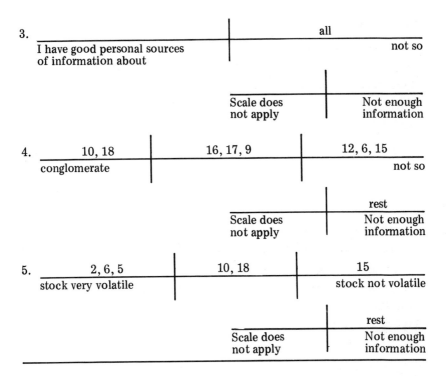

Questionnaire 2, which included his unique set of raw attribute labels.

## 7. Instructions to Questionnaire 3

**Questionnaire 3**

*Introduction*
Though brief, this questionnaire is the key to modeling the relation of your criteria to your preferences. It is acceptable to fill it out either directly after Questionnaire 2 or within the next day or two.

*Directions*

I. Part One

You are to prepare the accompanying list of stocks by ordering them from most suitable to least suitable for the one particular objective you choose below. (Unless you are an individual investor, choose the objective most typically employed by you in your work.)

*Objectives* (Check one or write in)

[ ]   very short-term trading (long)

[ ]   short-term speculation (long)

[ ]   intermediate term capital appreciation with above-average risk

[ ]   long-term capital appreciation with above-average risk

[ ]   long-term capital appreciation and safety, income to be re-invested

[ ]   safety and dividend income

[ ]   dividend income with chance for good capital appreciation

[ ]   other (write in) _____

*Example*

| Column 1 | Column 2 | Column 3 Ranking (Most Suitable) | Column 4 Scaling (Extremely Suitable) |
|---|---|---|---|
| Riegel | Safeway | Safeway | |
| Revlon | Revlon | Revlon | |
| Safeway | Riegel | Riegel | |
| Sanders Ass. | Sanders | Sanders | |
| Roan Sel. | Roan | Roan | |
| | | (Least Suitable) | (Extremely Unsuitable) |

Rank the accompanying list of common stocks from most to least suitable, placing the re-ordered list in column 3. Use columns 1 and 2 as work space for trial rankings. You may use either the identifying numbers or abbreviations of the names of stocks. After column 3 has been completed, assign a score for each stock on the scale in column 4 by marking a line from the stock to its place on the scale. All stocks must be ranked and scaled, even if you know little about them.

**8. Two Typical Subjects' Responses to Questionnaire 3**
On the following pages are responses obtained from Subject 30, a junior investment officer who was successfully modeled, and Subject 23, an individual investor who was *not* successfully modeled.

**9. List of Stocks Used in Questionnaires 2 and 3**
See page 90.

**10. List of Stocks Used in Questionnaires 4 and 5**
See page 113.

*Part I  Actual Exercise*

(Fill in using accompanying list of twenty stocks)

| Column 1 | Column 2 Workspace | Column 3 Ranking (Most Suitable) | Column 4 Scaling (Extremely Suitable) |
|---|---|---|---|
| | | Sperry Rand | |
| $^{sr}$Mag | | Magnavox | |
| CI Uac | | Amer. Mach. Fdy. | |
| Var | | City Investing | |
| Four Seas | | ITT | |
| | | United Aircraft | |
| Delta | | RCA | |
| fair | | S.O. Jersey | |
| GE | | Gen. Elec. | |
| loews | | Varian | |
| Pac Pet RCA | | Four Seasons | |
| SOJ | | Delta Air. | |
| | | Loews | |
| | | Fairchild | |
| Monsanto | | Brunswick | |
| Dymo | | Pacific Pet. | |
| Am | | Monsanto | |
| Anac | | Anaconda | |
| | | Dymo | |
| | | Amer. Motors | |
| | | (Least Suitable) | (Extremely Unsuitable) |

*Part I  Actual Exercise*

(Fill in using accompanying list of twenty stocks)

| Column 1 | Column 2 Workspace | Column 3 Ranking (Most Suitable) | Column 4 Scaling (Extremely Suitable) |
|---|---|---|---|
| ——— | ——— | ——— | — — |
| ——— | ——— | ——— | |
| ——— | ——— | ——— | — — |
| ——— | ——— | ——— | — — |
| ——— | ——— | ——— | — — |
| ——— | ——— | ——— | — — |
| ——— | ——— | [Rest] | — — |
| ——— | ——— | Pac. Petrol. | |
| ——— | ——— | Loew's | — — |
| ——— | ——— | City Investing | Neutral |
| ——— | ——— | Four Seasons | |
| ——— | ——— | Dymo | — — |
| ——— | ——— | Delta | |
| ——— | ——— | Anaconda | — — |
| ——— | ——— | Brunswick | |
| ——— | ——— | ——— | — — |
| ——— | ——— | ——— | — — |
| ——— | ——— | ——— | — — |
| ——— | ——— | ——— | — — |
| ——— | ——— | ——— | |
| ——— | ——— | (Least Suitable) | (Extremely Unsuitable) |

uncertain

Individual Factor Analysis
                                      Results


This appendix describes factor structures for 24 of the 39 decision-makers who completed Questionnaire 1. A more extensive
record may be found in Wilcox (1970). Only those factors whose
eigenvalues passed the significance test described in Chapter 5 are
given. Within these, only factor loadings greater or equal to .70 are
shown here.[1] The relative importance of a factor can be judged by
dividing its eigenvalue $E$ by the total number of raw data attributes rated by the subject, $n$. This quantity $E/n$ gives the proportion of the total normalized variance of all the raw attributes
which is explainable by the factor. The *left* pole of each factor
represents a high score, the *right* pole a low score, on the factor
measure as used as an explanatory variable in the predictive equations shown in Appendix D. Starred (*) attributes were omitted in
later questionnaires.

The decision-makers have been classified into market participant types based on very informal information regarding their
institutional roles. This classification, shown in Table C.1, should
not be regarded as definitive.

1. The factor loading represents the correlation of the factor score with the
coded scores on the raw attribute shown.

Table C.1.
Selected Subjects Classified by Participant Type

| Subject | Individual Investor | Large Fund Portfolio Manager or Senior Investment Officer | Individual Trust Officer | Security Analyst or Junior Investment Officer | Quantitative Investment Analyst | Professional Trader |
|---|---|---|---|---|---|---|
| 3 | | | | 3 | | |
| 4 | | | | | 4 | |
| 5 | | | | | 5 | |
| 7 | | | | | | 7 |
| 12 | | 12 | | | | |
| 13 | 13 | | | | | |
| 14 | 14 | | | | | |
| 15 | | 15 | | | | |
| 16 | 16 | | | | | |
| 17 | 17 | | | | | |
| 19 | 19 | | | | | |
| 20 | 20 | | | | | |
| 22 | 22 | | | | | |
| 23 | 23 | | | | | |
| 24 | | | | 24 | | |
| 26 | | | 26 | | | |
| 27 | | 27 | | | | |
| 28 | | | 28 | | | |
| 29 | | | 29 | | | |
| 30 | | | | 30 | | |
| 31 | | 31 | | | | |
| 35 | | 35 | | | | |
| 38 | | 38 | | | | |
| 40 | | | | 40 | | |

Table C.2.
Factor Loadings Greater than 0.7 for Selected Subjects

**Part 1. Professional Trader**

**Subject 07** $n$ = 30

**Factor I** $E$ = 5.2

| | |
|---|---|
| .89 not so | research and development oriented |
| .87 profit growth probably the result of many favorable factors | one or two internal factors that would dramatically affect profits |
| *.84 not so | would buy for technological reasons |
| .83 "out" of vogue | in vogue |

**Factor II** $E$ = 5.4

| | |
|---|---|
| .72 large capitalization | small capitalization |
| .81 high trading volume | low trading volume |
| .72 stock not likely to ever be in or "out" of vogue | stock subject to sharp changes depending on whether it's in or "out" of vogue |
| .71 not so | company's product an existing or emerging necessity for a large market |
| .90 interest is mainly local around geographical area of company | widespread and active interest |
| *.89 not so | could anticipate under certain circumstances large volume |

**Factor IV** $E$ = 4.0

| | |
|---|---|
| .89 take-over candidate | not so |
| .78 not so | price takes wide swings |

**Factor V** $E$ = 3.6

| | |
|---|---|
| .87 trading vehicle, always some buyers and sellers | one-way stock — everyone is selling or everyone is buying |
| .75 would take large volume to move price far | can move tremendously on very small volume |
| .75 no thinness of market | thinness of market |

## Part 2. Mutual Fund Portfolio Managers

Subject 12 $n$ = 36 (Eigenvalues not calculated because Questionnaire 2 not completed)

### Factor I

| | |
|---|---|
| .92 earnings have been unpredictable | earnings have been predictable |
| .70 high operating leverage | low operating leverage |
| .72 great number of variables which could swing earnings drastically and unexpectedly | no such influences |
| .75 unclear what earnings growth will be over next few years | good apparent predictability of earnings growth over next few years |
| .88 not so | management has a record of reliable earnings forecast |

### Factor II

| | |
|---|---|
| .88 not so | operating in a strong market for its product |
| .79 current earnings projections unfavorable | current earnings projections favorable |
| .89 low projected rate of growth | high projected rate of growth |

### Factor III

| | |
|---|---|
| .85 thin capitalization, not very marketable | very marketable |
| .86 small | large |
| .85 little information is available | much information is available |
| .77 not so | I know many facts about company |

### Factor IV

| | |
|---|---|
| *.86 not so | beneficiaries of residential building activity |
| .90 not so | will strongly benefit from broad economic forces |

### Factor V

| | |
|---|---|
| .84 in diverse industries | in single industry |
| *.72 not so | explosive upward potential of stock |

Table C.2. (cont.)
Factor Loadings Greater than 0.7 for Selected Subjects

**Factor VI**

| | |
|---|---|
| .91 low historical rate of growth | high historical rate of growth |

**Factor VII**

| | |
|---|---|
| .78 not so | management will tell you what is happening |

**Factor VIII**

| | |
|---|---|
| .78 in a depressed industry | in an industry enjoying good business |

**Factor IX**

| | |
|---|---|
| .83 stock price not volatile | stock price volatile |

**Subject 15** $n = 45$

**Factor I** $E = 5.9$

| | |
|---|---|
| .83 small | large |
| .90 thin market for stock | highly marketable |
| .88 not well known | wide investment following |
| .83 not so | substantial assets |

**Factor II** $E = 6.2$

| | |
|---|---|
| .89 variable growth | steady growth |
| .71 speculative | not speculative |
| .91 future growth in revenues is unpredictable | future revenue growth is quite predictable |
| .81 not so | predictable earnings outlook |

**Factor III** $E = 4.4$

| | |
|---|---|
| .91 stock price well above highs of two years ago | stock price well below highs of two years ago |
| .75 stock has risen more than I expected over last year | stock price has fallen more than I expected over last year |
| .85 not so | engaged in government business |

**Factor VIII** $E$ = 4.5

.71 unfavorable stock performers         favorable stock performers over
    over last 5 years                    last 5 years

.85 not well managed for its industry    very well managed for its industry

.74 poor historical growth record        good historical growth record

**Subject 38** $n$ = 40

**Factor I** $E$ = 7.5

.88 stock has appreciated a great deal   stock has declined a great deal
    recently                             recently

*.74 we have been successful in          we have been unsuccessful in

.97 is a very fashionable stock at       presently in market disfavor
    present

.87 not so                               viewed as a conglomerate

.95 made new highs for the year very     closer to its lows than its highs
    recently                             for the year

*.94 attitudes have *not* hardened       attitudes have hardened against it
    against it

.74 not so                               cash heavy

**Factor II** $E$ = 5.3

.91 so vast it's beyond comprehension,   not so
    predictable

.91 stock price based on dividends       not so

.76 company less aggressively            company more aggressively
    managing its assets than in the      managing its assets than in the
    past                                 past

.74 old style, sleepy                    not so

**Factor IV** $E$ = 4.7

*.90 not so                              a real-estate play

.86 not so                               a leisure-time, recreation stock

.72 presently losing money               presently very profitable

**Factor V** $E$ = 3.3

.97 high multiple, high technology       not so
    stock

*.97 open-ended growth potential         growth has some delimiting
                                         factor

Table C.2. (cont.)
Factor Loadings Greater than 0.7 for Selected Subjects

**Part 3. Senior Trust Investment Officers**

**Subject 27** $n$ = 27

**Factor I** $E$ = 7.8

| | |
|---|---|
| .75 possible take-over or merger candidate | not so |
| .91 in uninteresting fields with poor growth possibilities | in interesting fields with good growth possibilities |
| .85 management has a poor track record | management has a good track record, good average annual earnings growth rate |
| .89 not innovative management | innovative management |
| *.86 low potential for long-term growth | high potential for long-term growth |
| .84 high yield | low yield |
| .71 low P/E | high P/E |

**Factor II** $E$ = 5.3

| | |
|---|---|
| .83 former popular "performance" stock now down | has been unpopular but I see reasons for hope |
| .81 I know little about | I know much about |
| *.89 great uncertainty in outlook for company | little uncertainty in outlook for company |
| .75 new management | not so |

**Subject 31** $n$ = 33

**Factor I** $E$ = 10.5

| | |
|---|---|
| .76 management owns little stock | management owns a lot of stock |
| *.90 has low annual growth potential | has high annual growth potential |
| .90 low P/E | very high P/E |
| .93 not so | management has made moves to insure above-average growth |
| .79 weak sales organization | strong sales organization |
| .92 poor record of long-term growth | good record of long-term growth |
| .94 not so | has unique product with great potential demand |

.71 has been too much capacity but demand is moving toward balance

has been too little capacity but supply is moving toward balance

.95 has low return on invested capital

has high return on invested capital

**Factor II** $E$ = 5.1

*.91 stock had sharp decline but has recently recovered somewhat

stock had big run-up but has sunk back recently

.81 stock depressed because of temporary troubles

stock inflated because of temporary success

.71 not so

participating in a stock market fad

.85 stock price has fallen off considerably recently

stock price has risen considerably recently

.84 recent earnings much below expectations

recent earnings much above expectations

**Factor III** $E$ = 4.2

.84 high quality

low quality

.78 I do buy current story on future earnings increases

I don't buy current story on future earnings increases

.81 grows at steady pace

irregular growth pattern

**Subject 35** $n$ = 29

**Factor I** $E$ = 11.6

*.93 weak management

sound management

.76 in highly competitive product lines with low margins

in sound product lines with healthy margins

.82 not so

in good potential growth areas

.89 poor earnings record for past ten years

good earnings record for past ten years

*.93 not so

management has made better moves than company's industry as a whole over last ten years

.94 not so

has a close knowledge of their customers' needs

.87 not an innovator

innovator

.71 in cyclical industry

not so

*.87 in a weak industry

in a strong industry

*.93 has poor ability to capitalize on long-term potential

has good ability to capitalize on long-term potential

Table C.2. (cont.)
Factor Loadings Greater than 0.7 for Selected Subjects

| | |
|---|---|
| .83 not so | consistent performer over ten year period |
| .71 sells commodity products and services | sells specialized products and services |
| *.89 management lacks foresight | management has great foresight |

Factor II $E$ = 3.1

| | |
|---|---|
| .90 has blue-chip reputation | not so |
| .87 large | small |
| .90 well known | not well known |

**Part 4.  Trust Officers**

**Subject 26** $n$ = 26

Factor I $E$ = 8.2

| | |
|---|---|
| .80 not so | glamor growth stock |
| .85 has been an unexceptional stock performer | has been an exceptional stock performer |
| *.83 poor management | capable management |
| .80 a former market favorite which has fallen out of grace | not so |
| *.91 has been a disappointment | has not been a disappointment |
| .74 low P/E | high P/E |
| .78 not so | a management play, management has demonstrated ability to grow |
| .80 way down from all-time highs | near all-time highs |

Factor II $E$ = 3.6

| | |
|---|---|
| .84 listed on major exchange | over the counter |

Factor III $E$ = 3.8

| | |
|---|---|
| .93 little potential for very high growth rate | high potential for very high growth rate |
| .76 earnings stalled | earnings growing rapidly |

Factor IV $E$ = 3.0

.70 in dull area                              in interesting concept area, in an
                                              industry which will be in demand
.79 in an old industry                        in a new industry


Subject 28 $n$ = 31

Factor I $E$ = 7.2

.76 stock extremely volatile                  stock not volatile
*.79 low quality                              high quality
.77 management incapable                      capable management
.86 questionable management                   honest management
.77 company reports not lived up to           conservative company reports
.79 short history                             long history
.80 small                                     large
*.88 in possibly exciting field but           not so
    future is uncertain

Factor II $E$ = 3.0

.80 not so                                    serves a market for which demand is
                                              increasing rapidly
.73 low P/E                                   high P/E
.75 yields good dividend income               yields low dividend income

Factor III $E$ = 3.6

*.93 cyclical                                 not cyclical
.77 in an industry which has had too          not so
    much capacity but is crossing
    over into high profit
.90 for the first time in years               not so
    company will service market
    experiencing above-average
    growth

Factor IV $E$ = 4.8

.89 no story or the story has little          the favorable story about this stock is
    real substance                            good, points to underlying events
.73 a specific negative factor is             a specific positive factor is affecting
    affecting them right now                  them right now

Table C.2. (cont.)
Factor Loadings Greater than 0.7 for Selected Subjects
| | |
|---|---|
| .74 in industry losing charisma | in industry gaining charisma as indicated by number of reports, people talking about it |
| .86 recent market action indicates distribution | recent market action indicates accumulation |

Factor VII $E$ = 3.9
| | |
|---|---|
| *.79 I have done poorly in | I have done well in |
| .89 I think specific factor depressing stock is temporary | I think specific factor inflating stock is temporary |

Subject 29 $n$ = 33

Factor I $E$ = 7.0
| | |
|---|---|
| .80 in a young or dynamic industry | in a static field |
| *.92 price high relative to company's normal earnings pattern | price low relative to company's normal earnings pattern |
| .92 high P/E | low P/E |
| *.94 in dynamic growth area dealing with the problems of the future | not so |
| .95 earnings being discounted far ahead | earnings not being discounted far ahead |
| .71 in industry enjoying investment favor | in industry well out of investor favor |

Factor II $E$ = 7.5
| | |
|---|---|
| *.91 blue chip, high quality | speculative, low quality |
| .88 not so | have been involved in "fad" investing |
| .76 large | small |
| .73 product is a necessity, relatively stable demand | product is subject to fads, more risky |
| .86 old-line, well established | new, little track record |
| *.91 company is strong, well entrenched | company needs weathering, has come too far too fast |
| .87 future growth rate is relatively certain, assured | future growth rate is uncertain, risky |

**Factor III** $E$ = 5.3

.82 will benefit from lower interest rates — not so

.89 stock near its low for recent period of 6 months — stock near its high for recent period of 6 months

.89 has behaved worse than market lately — has behaved better than market lately

.75 public utility — not so

**Factor IV** $E$ = 3.3

.95 over the counter — listed on major exchange

*.94 marketability poor — highly marketable, specialist reliable

**Part 5. Security Analysts and Junior Trust Investment Officer**

**Subject 03** $n$ = 30

**Factor I** $E$ = 10.2

.93 large company — small company

.84 organized — entrepreneurial

.89 experienced, professional management — unexperienced, unprofessional management

.85 high intrinsic value — hot-tip, promotional

.70 established company — new company

.81 not closely held family management — closely held family management

.83 not one product oriented — dependent on one product

.83 blue chip — high flyer

.76 relatively permanent situation — high potential and downside risk

.76 decentralized organizational structure — centralized organizational structure

*.71 low risk this year — high risk this year

*.81 low risk next year — high risk next year

**Factor II** $E$ = 5.8

.82 markets not growing — growing markets

.84 poor potential for high rate of growth over next few years — great potential for high rate of growth over next few years

Table C.2. (cont.)
Factor Loadings Greater than 0.7 for Selected Subjects

| | |
|---|---|
| .93 low glamour | high glamour |
| .70 low rate of growth in last two years | high rate of growth in last two years |

**Factor III** $E = 3.2$

| | |
|---|---|
| *.93 does not operate in health | operates in health area |
| .81 highly affected by changes in disposable income | removed from changes in disposable income |

**Subject 24** $n = 40$

**Factor I** $E = 8.6$

| | |
|---|---|
| .74 very poor management | excellent management |
| .85 management has poor track record | management has good track record |
| *.73 management has not moved company into right fields | management has moved company into right fields |
| .80 has little control over product prices | has much control over product prices |
| *.77 stodgy company | remarkable record |
| *.84 poor financial management | excellent financial management |
| .90 afraid to use debt | aggressive use of credit |
| .82 growth is mainly internal | growth is mainly external |

**Factor II** $E = 4.8$

| | |
|---|---|
| .82 small | large |
| .85 thinly traded | broadly traded |
| .83 not so | has extensive financial resources |

**Factor III** $E = 8.2$

| | |
|---|---|
| .93 too much capacity in product market | product market is strong |
| *.88 outlook for greater oversupply | outlook for stronger product market |
| .73 low P/E | high P/E |
| .70 low growth rate | very high growth rate |

.72 stock has gone up and down        stock has not gone with the market
with the market

.84 existing product market will not   product market will grow rapidly
grow much

Factor V $E$ = 3.9

*.85 housing-related                   not so

.71 have some direct knowledge of      don't know much about

*.70 made money on                     lost money on

.77 construction-related               not so


Subject 30 $n$ = 33

Factor I $E$ = 6.1

.81 not so                             "concept" stock, product solves big
problem of the future

.89 not so                             has new management

.73 business is safe                   business is risky

.73 blue chip                          not so

.76 not volatile                       volatile, goes up a lot in good
markets, down a lot in bad markets

Factor II $E$ = 5.1

.85 cyclical                           not cyclical

*.89 in building industry              not so

.85 sells a commodity, normally        sells normally high margined
low margined products                  products

.83 earnings highly sensitive to       earnings highly sensitive to volume,
volume, operating rate rising          operating rate falling

.76 product has low labor content      product has high labor content

Factor III $E$ = 4.8

.73 not so                             growth stock — good earnings gains
in past ten years

.87 not so                             has fully exploited its available high
growth opportunities

.83 poor management                    good management

.70 not so                             steady earnings progression

Table C.2. (cont.)
Factor Loadings Greater than 0.7 for Selected Subjects
_____

**Factor IV** $E$ = 4.1

.77 low P/E                                  high P/E

.80 not so                                   I don't understand market's response
                                             to it

.94 P/E too low for long-term               P/E too high for long-term growth
  growth prospects                           prospects

**Factor V** $E$ = 3.0

.88 management more likely to be            management has high apparent
  "shady"                                    integrity


**Subject 40** $n$ = 40

**Factor I** $E$ = 6.0

*.89 inept management                        excellent management

.73 has made poor earnings progress         has made good earnings progress in
  in the last 1½ years                       the last 1½ years

.88 not so                                   the leader in the technology of its
                                             industry

.78 earnings/share growing poorly           earnings/share growing rapidly

.72 record the result of situation          record reflects management moves
  company found itself in

**Factor II** $E$ = 4.4

.87 honest, ethical management              management promotes stock

.88 manufacturer                             service organization

.73 I understand the company                I don't understand the company


**Part 6. Quantitative Analysts**

**Subject 04** $n$ = 40

**Factor I** $E$ = 10.4

.74 not so                                   large market following by general
                                             public

*.87 P/E not inflated                        growth syndrome high P/E,
                                             discounted far into future

.70 market action not volatile              volatile market action

.87 in making acquisitions would use cash     in making acquisitions would use stock

.75 low P/E     high P/E

.86 stock price based on sound principles     stock price built up on hope

.82 institutional recommendations     speculative

*.82 low risk, moderate growth     high risk, high growth

*.83 you could buy and forget for long period     needs to be watched closely

**Factor II** $E$ = 4.3

.71 not so     they are a major factor in their business

.81 not so     widely held by institutions

.83 not so     large following by institutional analysts

**Factor III** $E$ = 4.4

.95 over the counter     listed on major exchange

.86 thin market     wide following

**Subject 05** $n$ = 19

**Factor I** $E$ = 5.2

.91 low technology     high technology

.88 not so     computer field company

*.75 capital goods producer     technically oriented

**Factor II** $E$ = 6.1

.90 large     small

.92 little volatility of stock     high volatility of stock

.82 low growth potential     high growth potential

*.92 very low risk     very high risk

.80 established     new

*.80 large and old     small and new

**Factor III** $E$ = 2.7

*.76 has been a profitable investment for me     has not been a profitable investment for me

Table C.2. (cont.)
Factor Loadings Greater than 0.7 for Selected Subjects

| | |
|---|---|
| .81 I have considerable knowledge of | I have little knowledge of |

**Part 7. Individual Investors**

**Subject 13** $n$ = 28

**Factor I** $E$ = 5.0

| | |
|---|---|
| .73 earnings are down | earnings are up |
| .83 company has messy internal problems | not so |
| .71 management has not done much internally | management is energetic, trying to be progressive |
| *.70 company having serious problems | company having no serious problems |
| .93 poor management | company's manager is progressive, knowledgeable, and proven |

**Factor II** $E$ = 6.4

| | |
|---|---|
| .84 company has proven itself | not so |
| .73 not so | company in a hot industry for speculative growth |
| *.76 not so | has good potential because of its improved ways of doing things |
| *.77 solid company | not so |
| .78 not so | depends on the introduction of new technology |
| .71 fulfills traditional needs in traditional ways | major product represents a new concept |
| .90 low potential but certain | high potential but very uncertain |
| *.86 you wouldn't have to watch them | you have to watch them |

**Factor VIII** $E$ = 3.4

| | |
|---|---|
| .76 stock inactive | stock active in the market |
| .82 stock price has fallen in the last 6 months | stock price has risen in the last 6 months |
| .77 stock has already had its play | high potential, but has not yet had its play |

**Subject 14** $n$ = 27

**Factor I** $E$ = 7.4 ·

| | |
|---|---|
| .75 listed on a major exchange | over the counter |
| *.71 not so | new on the stock market |
| .90 well-established | some probability of not being in business in ten years |
| .94 important member of nation's business structure, large | not a corporate power, small |
| *.94 solid, substantial | not so |
| *.83 blue-chip | not so |
| .84 corporate health appears very good | I see potential threats |
| .76 I don't know much about price action | I have followed price closely |

**Factor II** $E$ = 4.6

| | |
|---|---|
| *.76 I held it, lost money | I held it, made money |
| *.82 large floating supply of stock | small floating supply of stock |
| .77 I know of no particular reason why they should do well | I know of some reasons why they should do well |
| .90 not so | I have some inside information on |

**Factor III** $E$ = 3.3

| | |
|---|---|
| .79 low downside risk | high downside risk |
| .79 not so | a "swing" stock |

**Factor IV** $E$ = 2.7

| | |
|---|---|
| .83 not so | stock has gone up a lot and then down a lot |
| .80 I have considered buying it | not so |

**Subject 16** $n$ = 32

**Factor I** $E$ = 9.1

| | |
|---|---|
| .85 narrowly based | conglomerate, broadly based |
| .76 small | large |
| .90 stock has no underlying price support | stock has strong price support, due to pension fund buying, for example |

Table C.2. (cont.)
Factor Loadings Greater than 0.7 for Selected Subjects

| | |
|---|---|
| .83 thinly traded | widely traded |
| .82 more risky | less risky |
| .80 in marginal position in its industry | in dominant position in its industry |
| .82 not so, speculation | solid blue-chip, accepted by institutions and investors for long-term capital appreciation purposes |
| .87 little known | very well known |
| .78 over the counter | listed on major exchange |
| .78 high availability to me of quasi-inside information | low availability to me of quasi-inside information |

**Factor II** $E$ = 3.5

| | |
|---|---|
| .70 currently in market favor | currently in market disfavor |
| .79 no single event on horizon could have large percentage short-term impact on price | single event has potential for large scale impact |
| .83 not so | stock price takes wide swings |

**Factor IV** $E$ = 3.9

| | |
|---|---|
| .90 has lost a lot of money | has been highly profitable |
| .77 poorly managed | very well managed |
| .86 low relative expectation of increase in profit in its markets | high relative expectation of increase in profit in its markets |
| .72 will benefit from a tender, merger, or acquisition offer | not so |

**Subject 17** $n$ = 34

**Factor I** $E$ = 3.9

| | |
|---|---|
| .80 I know little about the situation | I know something about the situation |
| .86 profit determined by very many complex and hard to predict factors | company has a relatively simple model of profit |
| .89 very diversified | single product line (broadly defined) |

**Factor II** $E$ = 5.3

.83 newcomer                                established, solid base

.86 not so                                  has substantial backing from mutual
                                            funds, investment community

.83 management unproved                     management proved

**Factor III** $E$ = 5.3

.78 high yield                              low yield

.86 not so                                  company is setting the pace in a new
                                            area

.74 low growth rate expected               high growth rate expected

.76 not so                                  logical take-over candidate, special
                                            resources or techniques in one area

.75 not so                                  now has important new products
                                            in the pipeline

**Factor V** $E$ = 3.9

.80 a past favorite of the market           a recent (3 mo.) favorite of the
                                            market

.70 had substantial decline in price in     had substantial run-up in price in
  recent past                               recent past

.84 being recommended as a                  not so
  turnaround situation

**Factor VI** $E$ = 3.6

.78 not so                                  erratic, wide price swings

*.72 not so                                 price reflects favorable expectations
                                            without good basis for predicting the
                                            future

.75 has low P/E considering its             has high P/E considering growth rate
  growth rate

**Subject 19** $n$ = 35

**Factor I** $E$ = 6.6

.74 serves declining market                 serves rapidly growing market

.73 not sophisticated in the use            not so
  of financial instruments

.87 growth record is poor                   growth record is good

Table C.2. (cont.)
Factor Loadings Greater than 0.7 for Selected Subjects

| | |
|---|---|
| *.82 has saturated its market | not so |
| .81 not solid | solid |
| .84 management not very capable | has very capable management |
| .88 not so, far behind competitors | moves into innovations ahead of competitors |

**Factor II $E$ = 3.2**

| | |
|---|---|
| .93 stock's previous lower level was from nonrecurrent event | stock's previous higher level was from nonrecurrent event |

**Factor III $E$ = 4.6**

| | |
|---|---|
| .93 not so | regulated utility |
| .73 diversified product line | single product line |
| *.85 not so | hard hit by high interest rates |

**Factor IV $E$ = 4.1**

| | |
|---|---|
| .78 stock has recently been falling more in down markets and rising less in up markets than others in its group | stock has recently been falling less in down markets and rising more in up markets |
| .93 stock has fallen rapidly in last six months | stock has risen rapidly in last six months |
| *.87 in process of being reevaluated downward | in process of being reevaluated upward |

**Factor VI $E$ = 3.1**

| | |
|---|---|
| .95 few factors affecting profit are outside company's control [or, regulated] | major factors affecting profit are outside company's control |
| .70 would be hard hit by inflation | a hedge against inflation |

**Factor VII $E$ = 3.8**

| | |
|---|---|
| .73 basic commodity product (demand not volatile) | product demand is volatile |
| .72 I know and have investigated myself | not so |
| .85 not so | involved in foreign operations |
| .78 stock price governed by real underlying forces | stock price governed by paper forces, incestuous rumors |

**Subject 20** $n$ = 38

**Factor I** $E$ = 9.0

| | |
|---|---|
| .82 low possibility of product obsolescence | high possibility of product obsolescence |
| .79 not so | has an important new product |
| .93 not so, staid | involved in computers, involved in new high technology products |
| *.86 has stayed the same | involved in a significant change from traditional behavior, or in a new entry into the product market |
| *.91 in a low growth field | in a high growth field |
| .72 stock not volatile | stock highly volatile |
| .89 not so | constantly putting out important new products |
| .74 not so | high management ability and willingness to move into new areas, with high cash flow |
| *.73 low potential, etc. | high potential for large short-term run-ups or declines based on a single announcement or on very little information |

**Factor II** $E$ = 10.0

| | |
|---|---|
| .78 new company, no record | old-line company, has a record |
| .85 small | large |
| .72 not so | large range of investors in stock, including banks, financial institutions |
| .89 weak financial resources | strong financial resources |
| .93 few people, management skills | deep management |
| .79 accounting gives inflated picture of earnings | accounting gives a very conservative picture of earnings |
| .84 ups and downs in earnings | consistent profit makers |
| .72 not so | consistent goals, good products |
| *.95 not so, less stable | has a consistent, stable image in the stock market |
| *.94 well below critical mass for sustained long-term growth | well above critical mass for sustained long-term growth |

Table C.2. (cont.)
Factor Loadings Greater than 0.7 for Selected Subjects
_____

**Factor V** $E$ = 4.1

| | |
|---|---|
| .76 sluggish, depressed kind of stock | rapid rising in up market |
| .73 sedentary management | active, aggressive management, careful assessment and capture of new markets |
| .80 has only occasional moderate shifts in price, dormant for long periods | stock has dramatic prices swings |
| *.81 predictable degree of volatility, or stable | unpredictable degree of volatility |

**Subject 22** $n$ = 34

**Factor I** $E$ = 4.9

| | |
|---|---|
| *.80 highly speculative | not so |
| *.88 low quality | high quality |
| .78 not so | considerable institutional participation |
| .84 thin market | has broad ownership |

**Factor II** $E$ = 6.8

| | |
|---|---|
| *.82 not so | growth oriented issue |
| .83 demand for final-use products indicates lack of growth | demand for final-use products indicates favorable growth |
| .88 serves a consumer market | serves a far from end-use market |
| .82 decline in earnings has occurred | high earnings growth has occurred |
| .77 fortunes tied to factors beyond company's control | not so, research oriented |
| .75 past performance has been worse than expected | past performance has been better than expected |
| .71 in highly competitive business where they are non-unique | in highly specialized market |

**Factor III** $E$ = 5.6

| | |
|---|---|
| *.85 short-term technical demand is weak | short-term technical demand is strong |
| .76 long-term technical demand is worsening | long-term technical demand is improving |

| | |
|---|---|
| .76 short-term technical demand is worsening | short-term technical demand is improving |
| .82 stock price has recently moved down by a large percentage | stock price has recently moved up by a large percentage |

Factor VI $E$ = 3.5

| | |
|---|---|
| .79 has a track record | has no track record |
| .86 listed on a major exchange | over the counter |
| *.73 [not a recent issue] | recent issue |

Subject 23 $n$ = 23

Factor II $E$ = 3.7

| | |
|---|---|
| *.80 not daring | daring |
| .93 bound to traditional customers | large concept of enterprise, looking for opportunities to grow creatively |
| *.89 passive | aggressive |

In this appendix, the regression models obtained from Questionnaires 2 and 3 by the procedures described in Chapter 4 are shown. The degree of validity of these models is indicated by the sample squared multiple correlation coefficient $(R^2)$ obtained from their application to the data from Questionnaires 4 and 5.

Using Fisher's $F$-test, one can gain some evidence as to the validity of the models even without reference to the data from Questionnaires 4 and 5. That is, one can calculate the following statistic from Questionnaires 2 and 3 data:

$$F_{k, n-2} = \frac{(R^2)/k}{(1 - R^2)/(N - k - 1)},$$

where $k$ is the number of explanatory variables, and $N$ is the number of observations. This statistic can be used to test the hypothesis that the population $R^2$ equals zero. When using the test on a regression equation whose number of explanatory variables is not fixed a priori, the proper $k$ for the statistic is difficult to determine. A liberal approach would be to use the number of explanatory variables actually appearing in the equation; a very conservative approach would be to use for $k$ the number of explanatory variables potentially available. This conservative $k$ corresponds, in this case, to the rank position of the last included factor measure in the stepwise forcing sequence described in Chapter 6.

The $F$-test can also be applied to the sample $R^2$ obtained by applying the model to the attribute data from Questionnaire 4 and correlating the resulting predictive variable with the actual summary preference data of Questionnaire 5. In this case, the appropriate value is $k = 1$.

Table D.1 summarizes the predictive models and furnishes enough data for the reader to make his own $F$-tests. Of course, these are more of an imperfect validity measure than an unconditional hypothesis test unless one is unwilling to assume the reasonableness of the normal multivariate model upon which the $F$-test is based. However, spot checks of the regression residuals in cases where $F$ values were significant revealed no unusual departures from normality.

The descriptions of the factor structures in Appendix C may be used to gain an understanding of what the explanatory variables mean; again, a high factor measure score refers to a stock describable by the left pole of the factor, a low score by the right pole.

Table D.1

| Subject | Q. 2 and 3 $N$ | Conservative $k$ | Predictive Equation | $R^2$ | Q. 4 and 5 $N$ | Validation $R^2$ |
|---|---|---|---|---|---|---|
| 03 | 20 | 1 | $Y = 710 + F_1 (1.35)$ | .51 | 20 | .25 but $R < 0$ |
| 04 | 20 | 3 | $Y = 1006 - F_2(0.95)$ | .56 | 20 | .26 |
| 05 | 20 | 1 | $Y = 418 - F_2(1.17)$ | .27 | 20 | .36 |
| 07 | 20 | 1 | $Y = 523 - F_2(3.11)$ | .52 | 20 | .67 |
| 12 | | | . . . | | | |
| 13 | 20 | | $Y = 760 - F_2(0.88)$ | .10 | 20 | .65 |
| 14 | 20 | 3 | $Y = 738 - F_3(1.30)$ | .29 | 20 | .03 |
| 15 | 12 | 3 | $Y = 1510 + F_2(0.73) -F_8(0.93)$ | .78 | 20 | .39 |
| 16 | 20 | 2 | $Y = 422 + F_1(0.07) -F_4(1.00)$ | .04 | 20 | .41 |
| 17 | 20 | 3 | $Y = 1781 - F_1(0.76) -F_3(0.78)$ | .60 | 20 | .25 |
| 19 | 20 | 3 | $Y = 1690 - F_1(1.54) -F_4(0.78)$ | .82 | 20 | .63 |
| 20 | 20 | 2 | $Y = 1279 - F_1(1.64)$ | .39 | 20 | .35 |

Table D.1 (cont.)

| Subject | Q. 2 and 3 $N$ | Conservative $k$ | Predictive Equation | $R^2$ | Q. 4 and 5 $N$ | Validation $R^2$ |
|---|---|---|---|---|---|---|
| 22 | 20 | 5 | $Y = 2873 - F_1(1.94)$ $-F_3(2.93)-F_4(1.54)$ | .60 | 20 | .61 |
| 23 | 20 | 1 | $Y = 549 - F_2(0.34)$ | .12 | 20 | .00 |
| 24 | 18 | 4 | $Y = 651 - F_2(0.67)$ $+F_5(1.59)$ | .60 | 20 | .35 |
| 26 | 20 | 2 | $Y = 543 - F_1(0.94)$ $-F_3(0.83)$ | .59 | 20 | .68 |
| 27 | 20 | 2 | $Y = 395 - F_1(0.79)$ $-F_2(0.89)$ | .29 | 14 | .34 |
| 28 | 20 | 1 | $Y = 294 - F_1(2.33)$ | .50 | 20 | .45 |
| 29 | 20 | 4 | $Y = 1388 + F_2(2.25)$ $+F_3(3.23)-F_4(1.22)$ | .87 | | — |
| 30 | 20 | 4 | $Y = 645 + F_4(1.56)$ $-F_5(1.17)$ | .63 | 20 | .29 |
| 35 | 20 | 2 | $Y = 1262 - F_1(3.14)$ $-F_2(0.78)$ | .64 | 20 | .37 |
| 38 | 20 | 2 | $Y = 348 + F_1(0.99)$ $-F_2(1.29)$ | .20 | 20 | .44 |
| 40 | 20 | 1 | $Y = 833 - F_1(1.20)$ | .43 | | — |

Note: The function $Y$ represents the summary preference data of Questionnaire 3.

# Bibliography and Reference List

Ackoff, Russell L. 1967. Management Misinformation Systems. *Management Science*, Vol. 14, pp. B-147–B-156.

Alker, Hayward R. 1969. Statistics and Politics: The Need for Causal Data Analysis. In *Social Science and Politics*, ed. S. M. Lipset. New York: Oxford University Press.

Anderson, T. W. 1958. *An Introduction to Multivariate Statistical Analysis.* New York: Wiley.

Arrow, K., and Debreu, G. 1954. The Existence of an Equilibrium for a Competitive Economy. *Econometrica*, Vol. 22, pp. 265–290.

Benston, George J. 1967. Published Corporate Accounting Data and Stock Prices. *Empirical Research in Accounting: Selected Studies 1967.* Suppl. to *Journal of Accounting Research*, Vol. 5, pp. 1–54.

Bieri, James. 1955. Cognitive Complexity-Simplicity and Predictive Behavior. *Journal of Abnormal and Social Psychology*, Vol. 51, pp. 263–268.

Bourbaki, Nicholas [pseud.]. 1968. *Elements of Mathematics, Theory of Sets.* Reading, Mass.: Addison-Wesley [© 1939].

Bowman, Edward H. 1963. Consistency and Optimality in Managerial Decision Making. *Management Science*, Vol. 9, January, pp. 310–321.

Bruner, Jerome S., Goodnow, Jacqueline J., and Austin, George A. 1957. *A Study of Thinking.* New York: Wiley.

Bruner, Jerome S., and Tajfel, Henri. 1965. Width of Category and Concept Differentiation: A Note on Some Comments by Gardner and Schon. *Journal of Personality and Social Psychology*, Vol. 2, pp. 261–264.

Clarkson, Geoffrey. 1962. *Portfolio Selection: A Simulation of Trust Investment.* Englewood Cliffs, N.J.: Prentice-Hall.

Cliff, Norman. 1969. Liking Judgements and Multidimensional Scaling. *Educational and Psychological Measurement*, Vol. 29, pp. 73–85.

Cootner, Paul, ed. 1964. *The Random Character of Stock Market Prices.* Cambridge, Mass. M.I.T. Press.

Cyert, R. M., Dill, W. R., and March, J. G. 1958. The Role of Expectations in Business Decision-Making. *Administrative Science Quarterly*, Vol. 3, pp. 307–340.

Dalkey, N. 1969. An Experimental Study of Group Opinion. *Futures*, Vol. 1, No. 5 (September), pp. 408–420.

Danziger, Kurt, and Morsbach, Helmut. 1967. Personal Style in Planning. *Journal of General Psychology*, Vol. 76, pp. 167—177.

Debreu, G. 1954. Representation of a Preference Ordering by a Numerical Function. In *Decision Processes*, ed. R. M. Thrall, C. H. Coombs, and R. L. Davis. New York: Wiley.

Dixon, W. J., ed. 1968. *BMD, Biomedical Computer Programs*. Los Angeles, Calif.: University of California Press.

Festinger, Leon. 1962. *A Theory of Cognitive Dissonance*. Stanford, Calif.: Stanford University Press [© 1957].

Fisher, R. A. 1928. The General Sampling Distribution of the Multiple Correlation Coefficient. *Proceedings of the Royal Society* (London), Sec. A, Vol. 121, pp. 655—673.

Francher, Raymond. 1967. Accuracy vs. Validity in Person Perception. *Journal of Consulting Psychology*, Vol. 31, pp. 264—269.

Friedman, M., and Savage, L. J. 1948. The Utility Analysis of Choices Involving Risk. *Journal of Political Economy*, Vol. 56, pp. 279—304.

Gardner, Riley W., Jackson, Douglas W., and Messick, Samuel J. 1960. Personality Organization in Cognitive Controls and Intellectual Abilities. *Psychological Issues*, Monograph No. 8, Vol. II, No. 4.

Georgescu-Roegen, Nicholas. 1954. Choice, Expectations and Measurability. *Quarterly Journal of Economics*, Vol. 68, pp. 503—534.

Glanzer, Murray, Buttenlocher, Janellen, and Clark, William. 1963. Systematic Operations in Solving Concept Problems: A Parametric Study. *Psychological Monographs*, Vol. 77 (Whole No. 564), pp. 1—50.

Glixman, Alfred. 1965. Categorizing Behavior as a Function of Meaning Domain. *Journal of Personality and Social Psychology*, Vol. 2, pp. 370—377.

Green, Paul E., and Maheshwari, Arun. 1969. Common Stock Perception and Preference: An Application of Multidimensional Scaling. *The Journal of Business*, Vol. 42, p. 439—457.

Harman, Harry H. 1967. *Modern Factor Analysis*. 2nd ed. Chicago: University of Chicago Press.

Hayek, F. A. von. 1937. Economics and Knowledge. *Economica*, n. s., Vol. 4, pp. 33—54.

Hayek, F. A. von. 1942, 1943, 1944. Scientism and the Study of Society. *Economica*, n. s., Vol. 9, pp. 267—291; Vol. 10, pp. 34—63; Vol. 11, pp. 27—39.

Hayek, F. A. von. 1945. The Use of Knowledge in Society. *American Economic Review*, Vol. 35, pp. 519–530.

Herzberg, Paul A. 1969. The Parameters of Cross-Validation. *Psychometrika Monograph Supplement*, Vol. 34, No. 2, Part 2, p. 1–70.

Horan, C. G. 1969. Multidimensional Scaling: Combining Observations When Individuals Have Different Perceptual Structures. *Psychometrika*, Vol. 34, pp. 139–165.

Hovland, Carl, and Weiss, Walter. 1953. Transmission of Information Concerning Concepts through Positive and Negative Instances. *Journal of Experimental Psychology*, Vol. 45, pp. 175–182.

Jensen, Michael C., ed. 1970. *Studies in the Theory of Capital Markets*. New York: Praeger.

Johnston, J. 1963. *Econometric Methods*. New York: McGraw-Hill.

Kaplan, A., Skogstad, A. L., and Girshick, M. A. 1950. The Prediction of Social and Technological Events. *Public Opinion Quarterly*, Vol. 14, pp. 93–110.

Katona, George. 1947. Contribution of Psychological Data to Economic Analysis. *Journal of the American Statistical Association*, Vol. 42, pp. 449–459.

Kelly, George A. 1955. *The Psychology of Personal Constructs*. New York: Norton.

Kelly, George A. 1962. Europe's Matrix of Decision. In *Nebraska Symposium on Motivation*, 1962. Lincoln, Neb.: University of Nebraska Press.

Klahr, David. 1969. Decision Making in a Complex Environment: The Usage of Similarity Judgements to Predict Preferences. *Management Science*, Vol. 15, pp. 595–618.

Kruskal, J. 1964. Multi-dimensional Scaling by Optimizing Goodness of Fit to a Non-Metric Hypothesis. *Psychometrika*, Vol. 29, pp. 115–129.

Lachmann, L. M. 1943. The Role of Expectations in Economics as a Social Science. *Economica*, n. s., Vol. 10, pp. 12–23.

Lavin, Milton. 1969. *A Comparison of Descriptive Choice Models*. Unpublished Ph.D. Dissertation, Sloan School of Management, Massachusetts Institute of Technology.

Lindzey, Gardner, and Aronson, Eliot, ed. 1968. *The Handbook of Social Psychology*. 2nd ed. Reading, Mass.: Addison-Wesley.

Linhart, H. 1960. A Criterion for Selecting Variables in a Regression Analysis. *Psychometrika*, Vol. 25, pp. 145—157.

Lunn, J. A. 1969. Perspectives in Attitude Research: Methods and Applications. *Journal of the Market Research Society*, Vol. 11, pp. 201—213.

Mair, J. M. M. 1967. Some Problems in Repertory Grid Measurement. *British Journal of Psychology*, Vol. 68, pp. 261—282.

Mannheim, Karl. 1962. *Ideology and Utopia*, trans. Louis Wirth and Edward Shils. New York: Harcourt, Brace, and World.

March, James G., and Simon, H. A. 1958. *Organizations*. New York: Wiley.

Markowitz, Harry. 1952. Portfolio Selection. *Journal of Finance*, Vol. 7, pp. 77—91.

Messick, Samuel, and Kogan, Nathan. 1963. Differentiation and Compartmentalization in Object-Sorting Measures of Categorizing Style. *Perceptual and Motor Skills*, Vol. 16, pp. 47—51.

Miller, George A. 1967. *The Psychology of Communication; Seven Essays.* New York: Basic Books.

Mitchell, W. 1910. The Rationality of Economic Activity. *Journal of Political Economy*, Vol. 18, pp. 97—113; pp. 197—216.

Morgan, Nigel, and Purnell, Janet. 1969. Isolating Openings for New Products in a Multi-Dimensional Space. *Journal of the Market Research Society*, Vol. 11, pp. 245—266.

Newell, Allen, and Simon, Herbert A. 1971. *Human Problem Solving.* Englewood Cliffs, N.J.: Prentice-Hall.

Osgood, Charles E., Suci, George J., and Tannenbaum, Percy. 1957. *The Measurement of Meaning.* Urbana, Ill.: University of Illinois Press.

Pettigrew, Thomas. 1958. The Measurement and Correlates of Category Width as a Cognitive Variable. *Journal of Personality*, Vol. 26, pp. 532—544.

Phares, E. Jerry, and Davis, William L. 1966. Breadth of Categorization and the Generalization of Expectancies. *Journal of Personality and Social Psychology*, Vol. 4, pp. 461—464.

Piaget, Jean. 1959. *The Construction of Reality in the Child*, trans. Margaret Cook. New York: Basic Books [© 1954].

Pounds, William F. 1965. The Process of Problem Finding. *M.I.T. Alfred P. Sloan School of Management Working Paper Series No. 148—65*. Cambridge, Mass., M.I.T. Press.

Quade, Edward S., ed. 1967. *Analysis for Military Decisions*. Chicago: Rand-McNally.

Rigney, Joseph W., and De Bow, Charles H. 1967. Multidimensional Scaling Analysis of Decision Strategies in Threat Evaluation. *Journal of Applied Psychology*, Vol. 51, pp. 305—310.

Robinson, John, and Hefner, Robert. 1967. Multidimensional Differences in Public and Academic Perceptions of Nations. *Journal of Personality and Social Psychology*, Vol. 7, pp. 251—259.

Rotter, George S., and Rotter, Naomi G. 1966. The Influence of Anchors in the Choice of Political Candidates. *Journal of Social Psychology*, Vol. 70, pp. 275—280.

Runkel, P. J. 1963. Dimensionality, Map Matching and Anxiety. *Psychological Reports*, Vol. 13, pp. 335—350, Monograph Supplement No. 3.

Schroder, H. M., Driver, Michael J., and Streufert, Siegfried. 1967. *Human Information Processing; Individuals and Groups Functioning in Complex Social Situations*. New York: Holt, Rinehart, and Winston.

Scott, William A. 1962. Cognitive Complexity and Cognitive Flexibility. *Sociometry*, Vol. 25, pp. 404—414.

Shackle, G. L. 1943. The Expectational Dynamics of the Individual. *Economica*, n. s., Vol. 10, pp. 99—129.

Shackle, G. L. 1952, 1953. On the Meaning and Measure of Uncertainty. *Metroeconomica*, Vol. 4, pp. 87—104; Vol. 5, pp. 97—115.

Shannon, Claude E., and Weaver, W. 1949. *The Mathematical Theory of Communication*. Urbana, Ill.: University of Illinois Press.

Sharpe, William F. 1964. Capital Assets Prices: A Theory of Market Equilibrium under Conditions of Risk. *Journal of Finance*, Vol. 19, pp. 425—442.

Shepard, Roger. 1962. The Analysis of Proximities: Multidimensional Scaling with an Unknown Distance Function. *Psychometrika*, Vol. 27, pp. 125—139, 219—245.

Sherif, Muzafer, and Hovland, Carl. 1953. Judgemental Phenomena and Scales of Attitude Measurement: Placement of Items with Individual Choice of Number of Categories. *Journal of Abnormal and Social Psychology*, Vol. 48, pp. 135—141.

Silk, Alvin J. 1969. Preference and Perception Measures in New Product Development: An Exposition and Review. *Industrial Management Review*, Vol. 11, No. 1, pp. 21—40.

Simon, H. A. 1955. A Behavioral Model of Rational Choice. *Quarterly Journal of Economics*, Vol. 69, pp. 99–118.

Simon, H. A., Cyert, R. M., and Trow, D. B. 1956. Observation of a Business Decision. *Journal of Business*, Vol. 29, pp. 237–248.

Simon, H. A. 1959. Theories of Decision-Making in Economics and Behavioral Science. *American Economic Review*, Vol. 49, pp. 253–283.

Slovic, Paul. 1969. Analyzing the Expert Judge: A Descriptive Study of a Stockbroker's Decision Process. *Journal of Applied Psychology*, Vol. 53, pp. 255–263.

Streufert, Siegfried, and Driver, Michael. 1965. Conceptual Structure, Information Load, and Perceptual Complexity. *Psychonomic Science*, Vol. 3, pp. 249–250.

Sugiyama, T. 1966. On the Distribution of the Largest Latent Root and the Corresponding Latent Vector for Principal Component Analysis. *Annals of Mathematical Statistics*, Vol. 37, pp. 995–1001.

Sweezy, Paul M. 1938. Expectations and the Scope of Economics. *Review of Economic Studies*, Vol. 5, pp. 234–237.

Taylor, Curtis, and Haygood, Robert. 1968. Effects of Degree of Category Separation on Semantic Concept Identification. *Journal of Experimental Psychology*, Vol. 76, pp. 356–359.

Triandis, Harry C. 1959. Categories of Thought of Managers, Clerks, and Workers about Jobs and People in an Industry. *Journal of Applied Psychology*, Vol. 43, pp. 338–344.

Tucker, L. R., and Messick, S. 1963. An Individual Differences Model for Multidimensional Scaling. *Psychometrika*, Vol. 28, pp. 333–367.

Tullock, Gordon. 1967. *Toward a Mathematics of Politics*. Ann Arbor, Mich.: University of Michigan Press.

Von Neumann, John, and Morgenstern, O. 1947. *Theory of Games and Economic Behavior*. 2nd ed. Princeton, N.J.: Princeton University Press.

Warr, P. B., Schroder, H. M., and Blackman, S. 1969. A Comparison of Two Techniques for the Measurement of International Judgement. *International Journal of Psychology*, Vol. 4, pp. 135–140.

Wiener, Norbert. 1948. *Cybernetics*, New York: The Technology Press and John Wiley & Sons.

Wilcox, Jarrod W. 1970. *Market Participant Cognitive Maps for Individual Common Stocks*. Unpublished Ph.D. dissertation, Massachusetts Institute of Technology.

Zannetos, Zenon S. 1965. On the Theory of Divisional Structures: Some Aspects of Centralization and Decentralization of Control and Decision Making. *Management Science*, Vol. 12, pp. B-49—B-68.

# Index